ANGELS EXPLAIN
Death
AND
Prayer

through Cheryl Gaer Barlow

ANGELS EXPLAIN
Death
AND
Prayer

through Cheryl Gaer Barlow

LIGHT
Technology
PUBLISHING

For more information about special discounts for bulk purchases, please
contact Light Technology Publishing Special Sales at 1-800-450-0985 or
publishing@LightTechnology.net

*   *   *

ISBN-13: 978-1-62233-008-9

Light Technology Publishing, LLC
Phone: 800-450-0985
928-526-1345
Fax: 928-714-1132
PO Box 3540
Flagstaff, AZ 86003
www.LightTechnology.com

Contents

The author, Cheryl Gaer Barlow, was visited by a holy angel of God. The angel touched her on the forehead and spoke to her. She was told that she was chosen to bring these words to Earth. This is why she was born on Earth at this time. What follows are the words of the angels.

Who Are the Mallbon angels?

We, the angels of the Mallbon, are the most sacred angels in God's domain. The Mallbon angels are the angels assigned to Earth, which is in need of our help. We will be with the people of Earth until the end of the world. We are unseen forces who are here to witness, not to judge. We are forever in the charge of God and do as he directs. The people of the world must know we angels are all around. No person on Earth is devoid of angelic oversight at any moment.

Were we not on Earth, this world would have ceased long ago. The angels are the true saviors of the world. We are at every movement of action. We are at every thought of the ways of God. The angels help in more ways than can ever be known to the human mind.

Birth and Death

When one has loved another so deeply and they
reunite in heaven, there can't be any words to describe
the intensity of the love
exchanged. It is more meaningful and more magnificent
than anyone could possibly imagine.

It is an indisputable fact
that the body dies but the spirit lives on in infinity and eternity.
The incomprehensible theories of the death of the body
are not valid. The soul is you. You live through eternity
to grow toward God.
Do not think otherwise, even for a second.
God is the name designed by the people of Earth to mean
the creator and absolute
intelligence. Come to God in all growth phases, and he
will not disparage you.
God receives all souls at all times with open arms. Most not only plead
to see God but
fall on their knees to feel the love surrounding God and the heavens.

A life in a body is a wonder, but it is not all.
This one life is not all.
An everlasting life is yours — with wonders you have
not thought to know. You will endure all things,
experiences, and feelings — all to bring you to God.

Introduction

We are meant to tell those of Earth that the death of the body is never to be feared. We are the Mallbon angels, meaning sacred. We hold much humor and are at rest upon Earth. We need nothing, but we act as though we desire things — not to deceive, but to help in ways not understood by humanity. We can manifest anything we desire. We help in ways unknown to you. We can live as humans on Earth. When we absorb the reality of Earth, we work God's wonders in ordinary ways. We will weld with your minds to create new moments of things not known on this Earth.

How to Weld with Angels

"Welding" is a word we use. We mesh with people in such a way that they can feel what we bring them in peacefulness — a softening of the emotions, with elements of love entering the heart. The heart is then stronger and better able to withstand the pains. The welding of angels will come to anyone who asks. Welding is done as follows:

- We surround you and let your soul be free.
- If you are in turmoil, we bring comfort and peace to you.
- We give you words to calm the soul.
- Your soul accepts this comfort.

If the soul begs for direction, we are allowed to weld the mind to bring a softening of the emotions. The words are needed to sooth the emotions. The soul may accept these words even if you cannot hear or see the angels around you. The words are integrated into the soul and mind.

This is a gift from God to the people of Earth. When the surroundings are not in focus or when you feel unable to cope with the people or circumstances around you, be still and ask God for help. God will respond to requests for help by mending emotions with aid from the angels. This is done by being aware of the angels. We surround you and bring you comfort.

There is an opening of the heart to release emotion. Tears may form. You may feel the movement within the body. When this occurs, the soul is open to receive the love from the angels and from God. We are trying to weld with the leaders of humanity. The minds of people must be cleansed by right thoughts. In the future of Earth, it will be most important to have right thoughts.

Most of the people of God will work incessantly to help others in ways not yet known to the people of Earth. You must, as a human race, lift the quality of thought to the highest level. When the level of thought is low and miserable, it is generated through the entire world. This affects all minds. When it is lifted to a level of joy, it lifts all minds. When you are open to understanding why we are with you on Earth, you will know that much help is needed here. Much help must be given to the people who are not in accordance with the thoughts and actions of God.

When a choice is made of what must be done, people often choose ways other than those of the highest thought. Our message to those people is to try to lift the quality of thought and deeds to weld with beings that will elevate you into joy. The lower pleasures are only temporary. People with little development of the soul will gravitate to the lower pleasures. Build your soul to its highest level. Let it grow and lift to God.

Angels Are Appointed by God

Angels are the love of the universe. We need only to lift souls into love. We will always be angels, and we will experience ecstasy at all times. We do not aspire to be as gods, as we are blissful in our purpose of serving God. A soul, pure and holy, may attain to become an angel, appointed and honored in the most sacred of ceremonies by God.

We have had this God always. We are angels to the end of the universe. God knows we shall forever hold this position as angels in the most high. The title "angel" is a word most holy in the eyes of God.

You are never alone. We are the angels holding the hearts of human-kind. We never weep, but we do feel its pain. We watch. We listen. We need only the welding of our hearts to yours to lift you and bring you peace. Ask us to come to you. Wait and be still. We will surround you with love. When you feel the torment of your heart fall away, you will know of us.

An angel is the appointed carrier of God's word. An angel is the spirit of God manifesting in a family of loving, sacred hosts of heaven. We work to effect God's plan for humankind. God appointed the angels. It is a glory to become an angel. We are thankful to be servants of God. We have the power of miracles. Some angels tend love and healing in ways that sooth people's sorrows and pain. The release of anger and fear heals the human body in a specific way. When an angel is sent to you by God, you are to be still and feel the presence. You will be filled with love and peacefulness. You can feel the love surrounding you.

Angels are always with you. We are with the soul that is you — not for a fleeting moment, but throughout your life. We want only to weld with your heart, to lift you into deeper joy. We work to communicate with you. The soul responds to our love. God will work through us to be with you and all people. We are ready to help you at any time.

Angels get directives from God to watch over the souls. You need only to pray and be silent to feel the workings of the angels about you. Prayer lifts the mortal thoughts to higher realms where the angels reside. Song lifts the quality of thought also. We listen and watch. If desires are in accordance with God's plan, they are granted to the souls. Prayer brings the wandering mind into focused thought so that we can better assimilate the desires.

Thankfulness Is the Most Powerful Thought

Giving thanks for what is given is a loving tribute. Your angels hover around you and know all things about you. When guidance is sought, the angels have a broader view to better help you.

When a soul begs to reach God, the angels surround it. A soul who wants answers to problems is comforted by our love. We try to soothe the soul and calm the emotions. A soul nearing death is surrounded by us as we calm its fears and lift the soul to a heavenly place.

The closer to the mind of angels your thoughts become, the closer the welding, and the more desires that may be obtained. You will be given many gifts and shall not be aware that these are given by your surrounding angels. All things given by the angels are given without need for thankfulness. To weld with an overlooking angel is a wonderful thing. The most powerful thought to give daily is thankfulness for all that is given to you. This act of thankfulness gives the soul a softness to receive more gifts. People hardened and full of resentment cannot receive because they are not in a state of acceptance for goodness.

When you know the teachings of the angels, no ignorance will be left in the soul. People will no longer be afraid or in pain. Now is the time to stand with the angels of God and help humankind.

Author's Note: Many things are disclosed in these writings. The angels aren't going to tell me every detail. I think I understand why. If there were no surprises, no miracles — if you died, went to heaven, and the irradiances, the magic of it, emanated all around you — you would stand there and say, "Oh, this is no surprise. I read all this in a book."

No, you want to stand in awe with your jaw gaping open! You want to be thrilled to your toes! You want your heart to leap so high, you can hardly stand. No, the angels won't reveal everything.

CHAPTER ONE

The Angels

We want to share with you how to weld with the angels. Weld by asking angels to come to you. They will surround you. Ask them to talk to you. They will share wisdom of great worth. You must be silent to hear the whispers. Sleep if you desire, because they may speak to you in deep sleep.

Even if you don't hear or see the angels, they communicate on varied levels that can be received and comprehended by you. The way the words are heard is through the subconscious mind. The wisdom can be received and heeded or not.

About the Angels

Do angels have wings?

No, the robes of angels are white, if they wish to wear them; but we can wear anything. You may see energy surrounding the angels as movement that appears as wings. When you create the image of angels in the mind, you will see wings. But we have no wings.

We do fly. The wings are energy seen by humans who determine it in their minds as wings. There is a movement of energy that could be interpreted as wings. The movement to weld with the minds of humans would cause sound in the ears similar to the fluttering of wings.

What is the light around angels?

We will tell you of the radiant glow around each angelic entity. This energy is the glow emanating from our beings. This glow is with the angel because it is all light and love. This is a physical emanation and a reflection of the beauty of the being.

We call this energy "crestone." This is not an aura. It is a field of energy given by God for angels to use in many ways. This is not a light and a sound; rather, it is a method of performing miraculous events. It is the power of God within and around each angel. This is a sight of heaven. This is not a sight of Earth. This is an emanation of God, a force, a power, a glow of God within the being. It is a powerful sight — a light, a sound, a spectrum of God.

The welcome of the angels is a wonder beyond imaginings. When this is viewed, souls are in awe. When the spectrums of light and color of the heavens are viewed, they are seen as magnificent.

Can we talk to angels?

Angels are not to be directed as the lower entities are. Angels are the messengers of God's word on Earth and on other worlds. Ask with a hopeful heart and not as a state of command. Request with humbleness before the holy, sacred creatures of God.

The souls of Earth cannot know the multitude of ways the holy angels help them in their lives. Give thanks for the blessings given to the souls of Earth. The most significant wonders can occur in the world through a humble prayer. Lift your soul and mind to God. Let the blessings come to you from the heavens. You will understand that you are more precious than you ever knew.

Do angels have names?

Yes, all entities have names given to them in the heavens by God. These names are given as eternal names to be used when the soul is returned to the spiritual state. All souls not of God are also given names. A name is the true self. The sound emanates with the reality of the soul. Each soul may reveal his name or have it remain sacred. We, the angels of the Mallbon, reveal our names to all who ask in God's name.

Can a person touch an angel?

You can touch us if we are in human form. God asks us to enter Earth to be his followers here. Many needs will arise soon. We help with the world's suffering. We eat and drink as humans. We sustain the ways of humankind.

We feel compassion in a deeper sense than you can imagine — not sadness, but love. We feel love in a much deeper sense than you can experience because of your being in the human body. We feel so wonderful in a life of feelings and so intense that tears may form.

Do angels have souls?

Angels are unlike humans even though we may physically appear as human. We have souls but not the same as humans. The soul of an angel is all with God. We are connected to God through the energy within the soul.

Are angels invisible?

The appearance of the spirit of the angels would raise fear in you. We appear to many on Earth. A light may be seen to let the soul know of our presence. The entities are all over Earth at varied times and are seen or not seen. The way the seeing takes place is this: the levels of the descent are made clear by enhancing the finer and more miniscule levels of being. As the soul sees the subtle levels, the spirit becomes clear. The most sensitive souls are able to perceive spiritual entities.

As souls are able to perceive spiritual entities, the spirit becomes clear. The physical senses perceive the gross states of the world. The levels of perception deepen as consciousness becomes more sensitive to these finer levels. Awareness by silent perception can be a way to experience the subtle levels of the spirit. The most delicate ways can and are meant to be seen one way to begin the mentions of the spirit.

Clear the mind. Ask for help to lift heaviness of thought and to perceive at more delicate levels. Be still and be aware of the angelic presence. The world is composed of varied levels of being. The more the soul delves into the subtle levels of being, the more these subtleties will be brought forth into everyday existence. The way tenderness is brought forth is to cultivate the growth of love.

Why are some angels alone while others travel in pairs?

When an ordainment is given, two angels are summoned to deliver this. The angels traveling together fulfill this decree. If two or more angels surround a person, it is to ready the soul for a change or a new beginning. Two angels who are with a soul since birth are to watch and confirm the growth of the soul. This is requested. The angels request that they both enter to be with the soul.

Angels are otherwise singular. We are in complete authority to enact our own bounderies. One angel is in wholeness and completeness. Angels ask to watch over the soul. This is given. Many angels are with each person. Only one is with a soul from birth through death, unless the other angels ask for this honor. One angel is guardian of the soul. Others are with the soul they desire.

The Power of the Angels

We will now tell you a story of a man named Melcote. He was a child of the war leader Wargone. The son Melcote was taken by the Hynulese and held for ransom. The father wanted to descend on the Hynulesetites to slaughter them, but he knew they would behead his son. He instead prayed to God for guidance.

The message from the angels came, telling him to let go of the anger and do nothing. He followed the angel's words and did nothing but pray for the release of his son. The Hynulese felt the love from the angels and were confused. They waited for war, but it did not occur. They let the son go into the land after waiting a long time.

The son returned to his father and asked what happened. The father told him an angel spoke to him and asked him not to invade. A hundred years went by before they took up arms again. The countries were at war until the angels interfered.

The story here is that Malcote tried to make peace even though he had been captured. A field of love from the heavens surrounded him, confusing the enemy. They didn't move to torture or kill him because of the confusion. The angels surrounding Melcote protected not only his soul but his body as well. The son of Wargone was so moved, he prayed to God constantly. The power of the angels is beyond human reasoning. This action changed many outcomes for centuries.

Ask for God's Help

How can we know when an angel is with us?

Earth's people are basically good. The more will there is to do good works, the more the entire world will benefit. You may feel your thoughts and feelings do not help, as you are only one soul. The mind and soul of one person can do miracles and wonders not only for that person but also for all.

Ask the highest angel in your realm to come to you. Ask humbly, for we are not genies from fiction but sacred, heavenly angels. We do not do you're bidding. Rather, we listen, feel, and try to help you. A feeling of love will surround you. A tingling of the eyelids may occur. The angels may be around you with a thought of bringing solace to your heart. You may feel a letting go of hate or fear. You may feel calmness as we surround you.

The way the angels listen to you is through your thoughts. Send thoughts of the highest import. Send love. Send gratitude. A soul only needs to feel thankfulness to attract angels. Thankfulness brings the light around you, which is seen by all the angels.

Feeling accelerates the movement of thought to propel into the world. God communicates through feeling. Let the people know the power that is within each soul. Humankind needs to let go of anger. You need to let go of pain and ignorance, and ask God to come to you. Angels will come to help. Those who ask for God's help will be helped. Open your heart to hear the words of God speaking through the most sacred angels. This will come to you now. Feelings of love, pain, joy, and sadness all mingle together in the heart of the soul.

We try to filter wisdom and strength through words. All souls want to feel happiness. Only some feelings enter the consciousness to lift these joys to humanity. To begin, sit silently and feel love and thankfulness. Everything will come to you in thought from your angels. This is felt by the soul. This is immersed in the heart. Love will be combined from peacefulness and contentment. Feelings of thankfulness will be immersed in an ocean of being.

Angelic Guidance

Do angels choose who they guide and protect, or are they assigned specific people?

This is the way we meet the wards of our purpose: We watch souls on Earth and read their thoughts. We see the light within their bodies. We choose the souls we wish to watch over.

Sometimes it is agreed before birth into the world that a certain angel will be with you your entire life. We know souls before they enter Earth. We choose the souls we wish to help. The way this is done is through observance of the soul. An angel may feel it can better communicate with specific souls. This is the choice of the angel. Sometimes the soul comes to Earth to complete a specific task during life. The angel is aware of this and will help guide the life plan.

Do angels intermingle on Earth?

Yes, angels can appear as people on Earth. They are as flesh and blood and can speak, hear, see, and behave as humans.

Why?

They are on Earth to help in the event their charges cannot understand a communication. They may appear on Earth to keep their charges from a mutilation or premature death of the body. At times, prophetic dreams or warnings, visions, whisperings, other communications, or strange feelings can be given but might not be understood. Angels might enter Earth to save the physical body until the time is right for the soul to leave it.

These visitations can be done to keep you on your life path or guide you the correct way. You, having free will, can refuse the guidance. There could be reasons that are not given to humans as well. The angels do not interfere. We only guide you in subtle ways.

All reasons for our appearance on Earth are not given. Angels can appear anywhere at any time. We are with many people who are not aware they are conversing with angels. Angels may not let the people know our identities. Angels help in whatever way is needed. We easily move between heaven and Earth. We are not on Earth to test people. We are only here to suggest and guide. We can ward off possible devastating circumstances.

The world is filled with angels now. The world needs our help badly at this time. We can appear or disappear at any moment. An angel may want to work many deeds before returning to the heavens. This can be done.

When you speak to strangers, they might be angels. Tell them of the angels on Earth. The angels walk Earth embodied as humans. We angels plan events of the future. We oversee the protection of our charges. We are to appear as humans and wear the clothing of humans. The people who have only asked requests of angels in heaven are now becoming aware that the angels are all over Earth.

If a miracle is warranted, we have powers to invoke the light of God. You may be in audience with an angel at any moment. We know your thoughts, your feelings, and your fears. We are here to oversee our charges on Earth. The world is racing toward new changes. Another world war is coming to Earth. Angels will be here to help the people suffering with the changes.

The Mallbon Angels

Who are the Mallbon angels?

We, the Mallbon angels, are the most sacred angels in God's domain. The Mallbon angels are the angels assigned to Earth. Earth is in need of our help. We will be with the leaders of the countries of Earth to infuse honor and truth. We will weld with all who ask for help in any endeavor with neither selfish nor ignorant motives.

The wonder of our presence is that we can help in ways unknown to all. If the people of Earth knew all the ways that helped, you would be amazed. We don't want to let you know all the ways you are helped because you would depend on us to do everything. We are not here as slaves or servants to the people of Earth. We help in our own ways. People must be free to live without interference from outside forces. We angels will be with humankind until the end of the world. We are unseen forces to witness, not judge. We are forever in the charge of God and do his mentions. A most wonderful life awaits those who hold honor in their hearts and minds.

Although the angels of the world are usually unseen, at times they are seen by people of Earth. We angels may appear at any time. We are the most respected angels of the Mallbon. We may do works of God in varied ways. At times, it may be necessary to be seen by humans. We can be heard as well — to warn or to tell of a wonderment about to occur. The people of the world must know we are all around.

A miraculous occurrence may be the work of an angel or many angels. Can one live a life unaware of the heavenly beings surrounding him or her? Of course, but to be aware of us will not only bring us closer to help you but also add dimension to your demeanor. All the angels in the world will be with us in the lifting of souls at the end of Earth. It will be a most glorious event. The most you can hear or feel will be at this event. Colors and sound beyond imaginings will occur.

The Mallbon angels are appointed by God. We are not an entity of the nonentities. The Mallbon are noble and gracious. The Mallbon were once souls who were given the message to have audience with the one holy God. We met the procession to see God and were ushered to his mention.

God appointed each of us to be his holy angels by watching our development through lifetimes. We are honored to be his most sacred angels. We were not angels from the beginning. We were appointed at different times. On the appointment, we were given directives and tremendous powers. We are here to be messengers of God's word. We are here to help humankind in all ways to grow toward God. We are here to evaluate all prayer and make decisions accordingly. We are here to guide our charges and to watch and protect their souls.

No person on Earth is devoid of angelic oversight at any moment. The Mallbon angels are a group of angelic forces assigned to Earth because of the tremendous need here. The Mallbon are the most sacred of all angel hosts of heaven. We can give peace and comfort. We can endure the pain and ignorance of the children of God. We can give fulfillment to waiting souls. We carry out the will of God with hallowed hearts.

No one need fear the workings in God's heavens or by God's angels. We will welcome all souls into heaven to see the wondrous ways God can express love for all. We angels are most honored to be in God's kingdom. We are the waiters in the heavens, which is not a lowly calling. We lift souls to heaven. We work wonders when they are needed on Earth. We love God and help the word of God be accepted on Earth. We will not falter in our methods. We make no mistakes. We are God's perfect angels walking the heavens and Earth.

Do your visits on Earth affect the answering of prayers?

No, not at all. We have visited Earth over many eons of time. The answering of prayers is affected by your sincerity, your feelings, and the way it would affect others. If we visit Earth to speak with you and you rebuke us, we understand your thoughts and feelings. We hold no animosity. Each prayer is answered on its own merit. We are not capable of corruption. We cannot be swayed. We are perfection and righteous in all ways of God. Should your daily lives be filled with a manner of dignity and kindness, you will have no concerns when you speak with an angel.

Be not surprised at the power of angels. We can do much. We can help in many ways. Let us help. We, as angels, want to help those who yearn for a closer life to God. We whisper to those who desire to be nearer to God but don't know how, realizing they may not hear us except with their minds.

Do angels test the characters of the souls they overlook?

The soul is known before birth unto Earth. The charge is chosen to be watched over. The charge's dreams are watched to see how the soul reacts to varied occurrences. The charge's life is watched but not judged. Tests are done during life to better understand the charge. When the choices show the true character of the soul, we watch. If the charge does work that is filled with love, we are overcome with feelings. It is much like a mother watching a child.

The love we have for our charges is so strong. When the soul grows toward God, we are elated. Your souls are tested many times during your lives on Earth. Your character is revealed in the ways you respond to trials put before you. When you do the right thing, putting your desires aside, your angel has cause to celebrate. The angel overlooking you will be honored that you have made decisions to prove your mettle.

The Men of the Mallbon

Who are the Men of the Mallbon?

The Men of the Mallbon are the angels of the most high. In the order, they are between the archangels and us, the Mallbon angels. They are communicators, and they hold meetings to convene all angels. There is much organization in the heavens.

Is there a patriarchy of males over females in the heavens or in the order of the Mallbon?

No, the Men of the Mallbon are only male; however, female angels of the highest exist in equal or higher realms. There is no movement to oppress the female in the heavens.

Are the Mallbon angels only female?

No, we are male and female in appearance. These angels weld to whichever is needed. Were we not on Earth, this world would have ceased to exist long ago. We angels are the true saviors of the world. We are at every mention of humanity. We are at every thought of the ways of God. We help in more ways than can ever be known to the human mind.

The love of the world is because of angels. The movement of minds toward God is because of angels. God's domain is reminiscent of their work of growth on Earth. The angels of God are to be revered most humbly. An angel is the most-revered, most-loved host of the heavens. God himself appointed the angels one by one. This is the most treasured appointment. The waves of love emanating from them are coveted by others.

Their compassion can be felt. Their words can be employed. They are the most sacred in the heavens and most holy in all endeavors. Give praise and love to those holy creatures of God. The holiest of the angels are assigned to Earth, as the people of Earth need the most help. We implore you to know that we are with you, beside you, watching over you. People of the world: Let your awareness open to the knowledge you are always and forever surrounded by angels.

Create your wonderful life from the passion within, and live it with freedom and love. "God" is the only word not understood by people of Earth. God is all intelligence manifesting in all form in any place. All wonders are his works. All lives are his. All creations of all existence are his. The worlds are his. The angels commune with God and with humankind.

A man of another world can be on Earth to help by simply sending his intensive thoughts. This will help in many ways. He is a traveler in many systems. People of Earth will be affected by his presence. When he arrives, no one will know of him. His presence will not be publicized. He will work silently to help increase the levels of thought on Earth. His name will be a secret.

When he is on Earth, wonders will take place. Yes, the thoughts will be so powerful. This can and will occur. The soul is now coming to Earth. Many travelers have been on Earth at varied times. They are neither gods nor angels but men of other worlds. They alter Earth's progression in positive ways.

We are always with all people of Earth but do not interfere with the wills of the souls on Earth. We are the holy angels of God, and we serve God, the Father in heaven. The ways of humanity will be and must be altered if the world is to progress. May these words help souls understand the importance of right thought. Catastrophes need not occur. Pain and suffering need not occur. People's minds will elevate to affect the world's occurrences.

It is not the wrath of God. God is all-powerful but also gentle and loving. God gives only love to the souls. If the body is killed, the soul is taken into bliss. This bliss cannot occur on Earth as it is now. A world of bliss is a long way from reality on Earth. Suffering must occur because the souls on Earth project lowly thoughts and lowly actions.

We are the holy angels of God. Yes, we try to help in many ways, but we are not to be used to grant wishes. The angels of God overlook life, the soul, and the body, but we are with you to help the growth of the soul.

The Angels of Earth

Do angels exist other than the Mallbon?

We only want to help the people of Earth. We are the sacred angels of God, appointed by God to be the most holy angels of all worlds. Angels are in all spheres of life. The angels overlooking the people of Earth are the Mallbon angels, the Wordon angels, and the angels of Nome.

The angels of Nome oversee the workings of people of Earth. They help in varied ways. They carry out God's plans, not only in ways known but also in ways unknown. Events such as wars, movements on Earth, and ways to be with the one God may all be workings of these angels.

The Wordon angels are so beautiful. These angels are appointed by God to glorify all worlds. These angels are the seers of goodness. They lift the hearts of humanity to see God in his glory. The Wordon angels lift their voices to sing to God. They are the angels who are now adorning the heavens. The Wordon angels are to be with God in the heavens, but they watch the world of Earth.

The angels of the Mallbon are the delight of all the worlds. We not only lift the souls of men to the heavens, but we weld with souls to bring peace and comfort. We surround the weary, the forlorn, and those marked with sadness. We bring the softening of the heart into love. We comfort all who are in need.

We are the appointed angels of God, the Father, to be with all souls on Earth and to lift them to the heavens. We are with all people of Earth at all times. We protect the souls. We cherish the souls opening their hearts unto God. We are the planned carriers of God's word. We speak to the souls of God's words, but they may or may not listen. We are with each soul through all activities. We watch, but we don't judge actions. We hear your thoughts. We hear your words. Lift to hear our words. Ask us to come to you.

We are the most sacred of all angels. This is willed by God. God lifted each of us from mortal souls and exalted us to be holy carriers. This was given to us by the one God in heaven. We were never souls on Earth, but we were mortal in other worlds. We are honored in his glory. We will be with God forever. Angels shall always be angels. Angels never leave the honor of the Mallbon. This is the greatest honor that can be given a soul: to be lifted to the status of the angels.

You will understand gods are to become gods after the growth of the soul elevates to that status. This is what the soul is honored to be in the heavens after all worlds and desires are dispensed. This is the ultimate growth of each soul, the ultimate intellect, the ultimate compassion. This will be done to all who warrant this greatness.

An angel gives its soul to God and becomes the servant of God in the heavens. There is no aspiration of growth to a god. We are selfless. We give all that we are or will become to the one God, the Father in heaven. We are angels into perpetuity. We are the sacred holy angels of God and do his bidding throughout all worlds and all eternity.

All things are gods. The reason we are the holiest angels is because the most sincere, most loving, most compassionate, selfless entities in all universes beg to be our mentions. We are with you on Earth as the people and animals there are the most needful.

One day you will know of us. You will fall on your knees to be in our presence. If you were aware we are with you every moment, you would be overcome with gratitude for our help. We want to stand beside you to help the regeneration of the world. The souls of Earth need the love, the thoughts, and the help you are capable of giving.

We watch and note all selfless acts on Earth. We note the sincerity of your hearts and your thoughts. Reach beyond your own needs, and the reward will be the opening of your soul. The soul is the sacred nucleus of God within each body. All individualism is contained within, as is all the love. When the body dies, the soul is received in the heavens. This is you. The soul is you. All souls can reach God by cultivating the love inside themselves. Angels are with you not only to lift the soul at the moment of death but also to help you reach the god-self in your soul.

The angels of the Mallbon rejoice when you open the soul to experience the oneness with God. Life on Earth is so precious. Be the person God desires you to become on Earth. We, the angels of the Mallbon, are always with you.

Higher Ranks of Angels

Who are the warriors in heaven?

The army of soldiers is an angelic force that abides in the heavens. Should any force move against God in a physical way, these angels fight to protect the heavens, all the souls of the heavens, the abode of God, and all the gods in the heavens. They protect the holy angels and all the archangels. No force anywhere can penetrate the soldiers of God. The soldiers of God are angels as a succession of warriors. They are truly angels of God. They are called the Chelton soldiers.

These angels will fight any predator of God and God's domain. Nothing and no one can weld the mind of these soldiers against God. These soldiers will fight through eternity if needed. Chelton armies are called on when forces try to penetrate God or his domain. Souls of Earth may call these angels to surround them during harmful times. They protect the soul so that the mortal may lift only to God.

The god overlooking these soldiers is called Zebreal. These warriors have taken the oath to serve God and give all to God. They stand with God and the heavens to protect from all predators. Wars against heaven have occurred. Zebreal and the Chelton soldiers protected God and all the heavens. No force can cause harm to God's heavens. Forces other than God exist. They are not to be given any merit or any worth. God will diminish these enemies. When this occurs, the soul is ended for all time in all dimensions.

This will not occur to God's children. Many lives of hatred and avarice toward all goodness must go on, and the soul must threaten God over eons of time for this to occur. It cannot happen to the living on Earth.

If you curse God and hate God, you will still enter the heavens. Souls who feel they cannot warrant life in the heavens are in bliss during the lifting. A soul cursing God will understand during the lifting of the soul. The mention of God in a hateful way will be no more. God will receive you and all souls as perfection, but you may remember actions and words from your life on Earth for which you will make amends. The soul will place itself in the heavens and plan to amend its actions that were not of God's way.

Who are the angels of the round?

These are angels of old, meaning from the appointments of the beginning. "Round" means these are the angels of the supreme and sit at a table in the round. This is a court of appointed heavenly angels from the beginning. These angels give the final utterances of the highest before consulting an archangel. These angels are the most profound, most intelligent, and most honored of all the appointed.

Can you tell me about archangels?

Yes, archangels are higher, closer to God. They are not the way you perceive them. They work in multiple worlds to help bring many closer to God. They hold the hearts of the multitudes. They do not wait to be honored. They work with God to mend the many ills. Their will shall be done on worlds unending; the creation of love appears in many forms.

There are great numbers of archangels. They overlook all universes. They are not concerned with individual desires. The wisdom and organization of these archangels is beyond the capability of mortals to comprehend. The archangels are charged with areas of realms, not individual planets. Groups of angelic forces serve each archangel.

Archangels are so magnificent. We bid to be in the presence of the archangels. They appear to us in tremendous light. They are pure light and love. They hold powers to change the future of worlds and universes. Can you even fathom the intricate workings of intelligence such as this?

They are all perfection. They can enact magnificence beyond anything conceived by man. They are profound in rulings, in powers, and in the significant workings of all. We answer to archangels. Their word is law and unchangeable. Their magnificence is intense. We honor them as one would honor a god. The intelligence of the archangels is above all in our realm. They know all. They see all. They hear all. They understand all. They hold power in all ways. When they utter words, it is done. We honor their words.

We want all on Earth to know of their power and their merits. They are all truth in all ways. They cannot err, for God's will is behind them. Archangels are, in every way, perfection. The archangels are at the feet of God. They will ever be the glory of the heavens. Archangels are not gods but rather weld with God to cause changes in the universes. They are angels who have been appointed by God to look over millions of angel forces.

The archangels are not men as you picture them. They are beings who look similar to God in that the light emanates from them. They are in the heavens and in all worlds. They can appear in many places at the same time. The power of the archangels is wonderful beyond comprehension.

Were the archangels appointed, or have they always been?

The archangels are angels of the highest. God viewed their intelligence and most sacred ways. God appointed them to their station in a most sacred ceremony. Archangels are the highest in the realms of angels. They are as gods in their angelic ways.

True Words and New Understandings

Universes are made of organized energy. All love permeates many universes. We are lifted through love. Each soul is purposeful in the heavenly realm as a unique entity. Earth is not permeated with love as on other worlds. The Men of the Mallbon do not have powers as on other worlds of existence. They oversee Earth but are not with the people of Earth.

The words we give you are the true words. These are to be given to the people of the world. The meanings of your words differ slightly from our words, but we try to speak so that the people may understand. The way to make the world understand is to bring the soul to knowledge. The soul will understand the truth when it is spoken from remembrance of what was known before this life.

People tend to give worth to documents from times long ago. When new knowledge is unfolded on Earth, people tend not to believe it. If the souls of Earth open the hearts of their souls to lift to God, they will know these words are the truth.

This will come about, and truths will be given and understood. A word of wonder is now given. The people of the world who know God will serve him in ways not done before. There will be a spiritual awakening covering the entire world. People will seek God not only for solace but also to pray for others. Most prayers are only for oneself. Now people will pray for the lives of others on Earth. They will lift their thoughts from hatred to help needy souls.

We angels will rejoice at the growth of the soul. When the souls on Earth beg to help and pray to God with sincerity and feelings, we rush to the soul and surround it with love. When the world needs hope, hearts will open to God. We watch all souls. The way the angels penetrate the human mind is through thought. If this cannot be accomplished because of unawareness, the angel may use other methods to communicate.

Many people wonder if the angels exist. Yes, we exist. We are with you always. All the days and nights, we look over your souls and protect them in a multitude of ways. An angel is with you all the days of your life. We don't judge. We don't condemn. We try to guide in unseen ways. A soul may or may not listen. It is a world of people who open their hearts to God and a world of people who heed only their own thoughts.

We are not to be diminished in the soul's mind or heart. We are not to be given homage as an archaic figure. We are living, holy angels of the one God. Ask God to bring us to you. We will be with your every action.

A life on Earth is so precious, so wonderful. It is a wonderful growth to be able to breathe in a body. Let your soul lift to God as you live on Earth. This can be a life of joy in helping and creating. Let the heart feel thankful for God's gifts.

We surround the heart filled with suffering. We encompass the soul with calmness and tenderness. We want you to know of our existence. We perceive our words as entering the mind, our feelings as entering the soul's heart, and our love as surrounding the body and soul.

CHAPTER TWO

Organizations in the Heavens

Someone who wants to reach God may do so with the soul's heart through feeling, through love, and through thankfulness.

Is there much organization in the heavens, or is it just all play for the souls of heaven?

When a soul enters heaven, it is in awe of the celestial wonderment. Things unknown on Earth — colors, patterns of design, music, writings, words, scents — everything is similar to Earth but so much clearer, prettier. When a soul begins to experience the heavens, it is one unending glory after another. The mind is in constant fascination. It is more exciting than any experience or adventure on Earth.

Wonders beyond imaginings await the soul. After a time of playfulness in the heavens, you may want to lift to a more meaningful existence. This will mean serving God as a worker in God's kingdom. The universe needs souls to help create, design, invent, and arrange all things of heaven and Earth.

It is pure joy to work in the heavens. As the soul gives in devotion and love, it can feel the more responsible ways of serving God. Joy is the normal feeling in all levels of heaven. As joy increases, a higher level of heaven is achieved, and you get closer to God.

You may design your own home as you wish. You may live in a celestial palace if you wish. You may live in a wondrous garden of the most beautiful flowers imaginable. When you realize you may create your life in heaven as you create on Earth, unbounded freedom awaits you. We help you create the most wonderful home you can conceive. When you reach the highest level of heaven, you can create worlds of wonderment.

The Men of Decision

The god overlooking the Men of Decision is named Weleton. This god is the judge of the Mothers of Question. The Men of Decision help to make decisions for troubled or questioning souls. Weleton is the final decision maker. If the Men of Decision cannot help a soul with its choices, this god is strong and most powerful. This god is definite. This god is not to be challenged, for he is the ultimate word.

This god is ready to tell the children of Earth to weigh questions carefully and to decide based on the outcome as far as they can see it. How does this decision change the lives of others? Are there better ways to handle the problem? Use your best intellect in decisions, not your fears. Ask God for help to lift you from ignorance. Do nothing hastily; decide cautiously and deliberately. Live with your decision. Learn from it. Stand behind your words and actions.

The human mind cannot know the repercussions of each action. It cannot see from all perspectives, so it must trust the soul, heart, and mind to do what is best for all from their particular vantage point. Make the choice. Go on from there. If it seems the wrong step to take, wait and do nothing until the answer comes to you. Do not waver. Stand and defend your action if it comes to that, but be prepared to take responsibility for your decision with courage and strength. The gods and angels are with you.

The Men of Decision are people lifted to the heavens chosen to help others make decisions regarding their future lives. The souls tend to lean into varied interests, and the Men of Decision help confused minds to focus. This is not a matter of vocation. It is an area in which consummation of goals will fulfill the soul. The most important message to the souls of Earth is that Men of Decision work with the angels of God. Their decisions focus on the expressions of the individual souls.

God appointed the Men of Decision. They will always want to help. The Men of Decision need not be seen or heard but can weld with your mind to help clarify your thoughts into purposeful direction. The Men of Decision are men and women who are under God's direction. These souls are servants to God for eternity. They want to help the souls of Earth, and they asked to help God through a communicative means.

A person requesting his or her purpose in the plan of God will be counseled to understand directives. When you create motives, you create solutions to these quandaries. Angels ask some appointed souls to help in areas of communication with the souls of people on Earth. The Men of Decision communicate not only with the souls lifted to heaven but also with people on Earth.

Ask God for help. God directs his holy angels, and the angels decide the best way to proceed in any action. If the Men of Decision are ordained to help, it is done. We angels now ask why many on Earth are not focused toward God but instead wander in chaos. The Men of Decision are your advisors in the heavens. They council the souls who are at a standstill in their choices. They ask the souls questions to help determine the most advantageous ways to progress.

This is a group that wants to help make decisions regarding the fulfillment of needs of the individual. They help in any way they can when a soul consults them. The love is very clear and pronounced in the heavens. Some souls feel love so deeply that they are in constant bliss. The loved ones want to be with them, but they are so overwhelmed at the love surrounding them.

The world is not aware of this intensity. It is the most incredible feeling one can know. Love this intense needs direction. The Men of Decision help souls focus this love and help them decide how best to serve God. God is with these them to help the souls in need of guidance. A soul in the heavens is in so much bliss, it may play in the heavens as a child forever. This can be done, but the guides will ask if the soul would like to help God. The Men of Decision help souls decide what way is most comfortable for them to create.

There are many, many Men of Decision. They are similar to high priests on Earth. They now want to help in any way possible. They question the soul to help guide it in the most appropriate direction. There are choices to be made. The angels are with the souls also, but we do not interfere with the soul's choices in any way.

You may do as you wish in the heavens. All wisdom is around each soul. Understanding permeates you. God is everywhere. Love is everywhere. The wonders of the heavens are everywhere. A soul enjoys this beyond anything experienced on Earth. If a soul wants to dance, sing, and play, it can do so. A soul can ask for its most important needs, deeply felt. All will be fulfilled as the soul requests. No one is left to be without love.

These spirits are very wonderful. They only want to serve God in any way they can. They are appointed by God to help the angel forces. They act as intermediaries between angels and humans. The human mind is on a lowly plane. The Men of Decision can communicate with these lowly minds of the people of Earth in languages they understand. This is not a matter of vocation. It is an area in which consummation of goals will fulfill the soul.

The Men of One

The Men of One are appointed by God to help in ways different from the ways of God. They walk with heavenly ways in that they can move through different levels of the heavens. They will not tarry in any heaven but fulfill their mentions and objectives, then move on. This is a way to help many who request council. They are men of God. They relate to men in earthly ways to be comfortable with them. They discuss the qualms one may have regarding the future needs of the soul. The way they do this is to ask the souls any questions they may have about their purpose in God's realm.

It is an honor to become a member of the Men of One. To be a member of the Men of One means devotion to the one, true, holy God of all that exists. We angels give great worth to these men. Women are also part of this group. When any soul has a question, they come to talk and help make decisions.

Many men in angel realms are called Men of One, meaning devotion to the one God in heaven. When a heavenly home is given, they lift you to the level of God. You are to place yourself there. They are waiting to help people. The Men of One are welcoming spirits to help lift you to the place you are to go when you leave this world. When you leave the body, the Men of One are the angels lifting you to the finer levels of the new existence. The Men of One are angels to meet and bring you to the place you will be in when you reside in heaven.

The Men of One are men and women who have lived on many worlds and are one with God, the Father in heaven. The Men of One have decided to bind unto god, not to become as gods themselves, but merge with the one God to feel his presence, surrounded by feelings beyond blissfulness. To stand in the aura of the one God is all these men need.

The Men of One are angels who come to meet you, and they bring you to the place you will be when you enter heaven. The Men of Decision will not want everyone to enter heaven before considering the choices available. They will ask each soul to think well about what it wants before entering heaven. They want each mind to think decisively before entering heaven. They will, even after this life on Earth, pull you to one decision or another. When you have a choice, they will try to help you.

All the angels will ask you to take a heavenly home. A ready place will be there for you. When you rise to this place, your loved ones can see you. When they help the angels, they can be with you. The way into heaven is not hard. We will lift all souls that have goodness in them.

The Men of God

The Men of God are the leaders of new worlds where we cannot be heard or seen. God tells the Men of God to let go of their old beliefs. He tells the women to now form a way for men to let go of the old ways and follow God directly.

The Men of God are people who follow God with devotion. These are varied souls on many worlds. They honor and serve God in many ways. Even Earth has followers of God who could be called the Men of God in some ways. They might not be ordained in the sacred organization of the Men of God, but they have sincerity and love in their souls. This will be given to them in the lifting to the heavens.

They live in a respectful manner befitting a child of God in all words and actions. They now resound this love in the heavens. These souls are worthy to sit near God and feel his presence. They are honored to be disciples of God. The demeanor of these Men of God is viewed and emulated by other souls. Their values are respected and honored.

The Men of God are God's souls who are in complete devotion to him. They are servants only to God. They wear the white robes of God's followers. They bow at the feet of God in total submission and devotion. They pray to hear God's words and carry out the most mundane of God's wishes. All is given to God.

The Men of Old

The Men of Old are souls who will continue to come back to Earth through many lifetimes. These souls wish to be honored as wonders on Earth. The old ones are old souls, meaning they are souls coming to Earth repeatedly for hundreds, even thousands of years in Earth's time. They will be the old ones who lead the walk with God in the end time of Earth.

The world needs the words of the gods and the angels to combat the ignorance within it. They are with you to help in any way possible.

Do they have powers beyond ordinary people?

No, they possess only great wisdom, so far beyond the people of Earth. They keep this wisdom to themselves. They live simple, contented lives helping humanity in small ways.

Are they aware of previous lives?

Some are, yes, aware of the past and of the future. They know what is to happen in Earth's future. They bring no notice to themselves.

Couldn't they help if they bring their knowledge to the world?

Human minds can only be influenced if open to knowledge. The growth must be from each soul. If truth is disclosed (as in these words), many will not accept the wisdom given. The futility is evident.

CHAPTER THREE

The Soul's Path

We wish to explore the ways that souls react to God and the heavenly entities. We will share a method of lifting the minds of humanity to the level of communication. We feel it's important that each soul do this in its own way and in its own time.

We want to be with the souls of Earth in this way. May each soul on Earth acknowledge that souls are of many levels. The spirit or ghost levels are common to the sight and the hearing. These are not to be seen as beings to implore. When these are seen or heard, disregard them, as they are lowly spirits and serve no good to humans living on Earth. They live in the light of Earth and do not know of God's light. They are not to be sought nor are they to be desired associates. The human souls of Earth are to try to rise to the levels of the gods and the angels they would like to emulate.

These are not to be confused with the souls that still walk the ethers of Earth. When these spirits enter to visit, tell them to leave your presence. The words they will communicate are not truthful. They only take action in order to make themselves known to you. They do no service to God or to humanity. Make your endeavors higher with the lifting of the soul and the mind. Seek to lift to the sweetest, purest, highest level you can attain. Give no worth to the ghosts of the lower world. Do not be distracted by actions of the lowly spirits. Many see and hear them. Give no merit to their words. They will only use your body or keep you from lifting your mind to God. It is no glory to be involved with the ghosts of the world.

Ghosts are souls not yet lifted to the heavens. They may remain on Earth after the body has demised. They may stay a few days or a few centuries. Some stay thousands of years. They stay until the angels come to lift them to a heavenly abode. They know they are in the spirit world. They watch others as they live on Earth. They do not want to be spirits. They want to be alive again on Earth.

If they can communicate with people living on Earth, they are intrigued and stay around that person. The information received from these spirits is not true or accurate, for they want to enhance the news they bring in order to ensure communication.

To lift to a higher level, talk with the angels. This is desired. Ask that the highest angel around you be with you now. Sit quietly and close your eyes. You might feel a tickling in the mind and the soul. Some may feel suspended in air. These are sensations of the mind and soul. Many will feel calmness, peacefulness, softness — a gentle surrender. These feelings will make you aware of being in the presence of angels. When this occurs, give thanks for their presence.

Give your soul to God. Let your feelings come forth. Let go of the angers and pains of daily life. Speak to God with the highest soul. You will know when angels surround you and merge with you. They will always be with you. When you need help, the angels will help in any way possible. Talk to God anytime. Talk to your angels anytime. Realize you are never alone. Your angels are always with you. Behave in a manner you would want your angels to view. They will not judge your words or actions, but they will know your thoughts, feelings, motives, and desires.

Now we will share a great secret. The way to lift to God is to work toward being an angel:

- View everything lovingly.
- Help whenever possible.
- Honor God in the highest.
- Be a servant of God.
- Send thoughts of love all around you.
- Make all things more wonderful.
- Create.
- Enjoy.
- Spread joy wherever you are.
- Adore God's creations.
- Be a sweet, gentle person.

These gifts are given to all who live on Earth. Many choose to ignore them to be strong, rich, and successful, but they are missing a chance to be close to the angels.

Lowly Spirits

What if you are not in a body? Can we find you?

We may touch, but nothing more than a brush is felt. We need to go to the mind and sooth the spirit. Often people are so upset that they can't feel us with them. We will watch until the anger is released. At that time, we come into the heart and mind.

What is the difference between an angel and a normal spirit?

We walk in God's light. We enter the human mind to weld the thoughts of God to the thoughts of humankind. We are the holy angels of God. We are not without God at any time. Spirits walk Earth as well, but they can be seen as having no power to help someone effect change. Spirits may try to enter your mind to send thoughts, but they cannot work wonders of God on Earth.

We walk in the light of God. They walk in the light of Earth. When you welcome angels, lift your heart to meet us. We will come all who ask. While spirits drift to await the lifting to heaven, they roam Earth, not aware of purpose. Many are on Earth. They do not behave as if they are angels of God.

We are the angels of God. We watch over them and the people of the world. We are appointed by God to become holy angels. Spirits of humans are not angels. Both seek to communicate with people on Earth, but spirits do not have God's permission. We seek to weld the ecstasy of the heavens into the minds of humankind. Spirits walking Earth have no power to do this.

When you see spirits with your eyes, ask if they are angels. If they are, they will answer yes. They will not answer if they are spirits not yet lifted to heaven. Ask the angels to come and protect you. When spirits are not yet lifted to heaven and not in a human body, they wish to be in a body again. They might want to go into another body on Earth. Angels protecting you will not let this happen. Angels may surround you to work their wonders. Weld your mind to ours. Spirits on Earth work toward coming to heaven, wanting the love of a world. We do not master any souls. The souls decide what is needed and desired.

The Importance of Welding with the Angels
What message do you want to give to humanity?

We want to tell of the most important plan to write a new welding plan for the souls of Earth. The world needs to realize the importance of welding with your angels. The actions of humanity may be changed from coarseness with help from the angels.

Sometimes the angels change the pattern of life paths in order to achieve a higher goal. If souls have surrendered their offerings to God, their lives may be redirected to fulfill the serving. This is not often noticed in life. You might not understand why undesired events happen in life, because you are being redirected for reasons only known to the heavenly angels.

Welding with the angels may help. The mind knows the reasons if only in a subconscious way. Your hopes are not always realized while on Earth. This may be due to an unremembered pledge to God, made before entering Earth's realm.

What was pledged to God will take precedence in the flow of life. The world will begin using methods to discover the mind's goals that were set before the birth on Earth. The mind must relax and be open to feel love from angelic forces. Be aware that the angels are always with you. Try to communicate with them by receiving the angel's thoughts. We angels are the followers of God in the heavens. We serve God in all ways. God's directions are carried out through our efforts.

The minds of humankind may perceive these thoughts given to us directly from God. Ask God with a humble heart to let you understand the directions from the angels. This will occur. A soul may not realize the importance of directed actions from the angels because they may not represent an easy path for the soul. Why can't it be easy and comfortable? The difficulties met by each soul are necessary for the growth of that soul.

We don't influence or weld in order to direct our will. We'll help the charge while we protect the body. We will go to the body to love and guide. Most of the help you receive is from angels, but you are not aware of this. All things help bring about the changes necessary to meet the new world. We meet to plan events and plan ways to help. All prayers are called into discussion.

We watch and walk Earth to help where we are needed. Children of God need not fear the wrath of God or the wrath of his worlds. Worlds without end exist. Some are completed bliss: worlds of love, worlds of creation, and worlds of joy.

Nothing is hidden from the angels, because we see the real you and understand why you do the things not of your worth. We watch the people of Earth, respecting acts of kindness. This is to be found in what is done and what is not done. This is to be found in helping others. We watch the soul trying to do right, trying to uplift humankind. God honors these people in his kingdom.

To give your own happiness for another is to love God. He is watching. We will not turn away from helping those who would suffer. We try to send love to the leaders of wars to let them evolve their souls. We hold them in our hands to tell them love can end the suffering of all humankind.

Let the angels see the life you've lived as dignified and respectful. We are with you at every moment. You will never be alone to bear your sorrows. One day, you will know of us. We stand with you and bring solace to your hearts. Now is the time to weld the souls of angels with the souls of humankind to make the world worthy in God's eyes.

The Omen of the Mallbon Angels

One mention is the omen of the Mallbon angels. The omen is obtained by the Mallbon as a way to distinguish the only people who will foretell the future, those who are given the words of the angels to see the future of the world. The words will be given in a lift of greatness. These people are followers of God. This will occur in a century called the renaissance. At that time, people of Earth will try to reunite the varied areas of the world. The most wonderful callings will come to these people at this time. These seers of the world will call all people to listen. The angel's words will then be heard all over the world. We will give you the words now necessary to give to the world; however, much cannot be disclosed for many eons of time.

The more pleasurable, more wonderful mention is the words of the great god Chapword. He is most hallowed. A home of the most worthy figures is projected unto the world. The way this is done is that the opening of hearts will lift the thoughts to encompass God. Then God's thoughts will be sent forth to Earth through the welding of the angels with humankind. In a moment, a word of God may be given to anyone. This can be received through thought. Let them know life is to be lived in fullness. Many lives are now to be taken from Earth, not to punish them but to bring them into God's presence. Many will desire to stay on Earth. This is because they do not remember the glories of the heavens.

In heaven, the god Chapword is ready to give these words. The most valuable presence on Earth is not human, animal, or insect life. It is the presence of angels. If they are seen or unseen, they are on Earth in fullness.

Making Requests

Can we make requests of our angels?

The most prevalent way to receive desires is to be open to the words of the angels. The way to do this is to sit quietly and ask the angels to come to you. Ask for the highest angels of God to come to you. Know they are with you. Ask the angels if they can help you. They will hear you and try to help. They may suggest ideas, which you will consider as your own thoughts. Let the soft words and thoughts of the holy angels spur you to make choices in life. The requests should be asked with a humble heart and gratitude expressed. The cause of the request is to be considered.

This is not a prayer to God but a favor asked. When you ask for help, it should be as if you asked a neighbor for help. Ideas will begin to come to the mind. When this occurs, the intellect will choose the best way to achieve this. Should the ways not be feasible in the mind, write the request on paper and ask the holy angels to help achieve this goal. Let the angels work on this in the heavens. The way must be clear for the desire to come to you. The desire must not be continually changed; the desire must be strong. No one can be hurt by receiving this desire.

The forces in the heavens will work to help you if this is a possibility in the life plan. We want our charges to live comfortably and obtain their desires. If we can help in any way, we do so. Words given in sincerity open the way to these achievements. Ask for help. Let the angels know this can be done now. Nothing is in the way. No one will be hurt from this action. Know this will happen!

Can you help us obtain possessions?

Many wishes are asked of God and of the angels. Our purpose is not to bring money to you. We want our charges on Earth to have happiness. The words we bring now will try to lift minds and thoughts. These words are not magic to bring all desires to you. These words are meant to bring you to God.

Lift your thoughts to God. Your life will be a reflection of the thought sent. Life stems from the sincerity of your soul's heart. Begin there. Begin to lift your thoughts to send love to others in need, and this will reflect back to you. Many wonders will come from this action. This cannot be pretended and achieved. Plans are to be made in the mind and physically enacted. Now the more intelligent decisions can be understood. The actions will come into fruition. The results can only be obtained through thought, preparation, action, and follow-through. This is the correct way.

When money from the heavens is requested, unless it is part of the life plan, it will not occur. The measurement of time is a quotient in this request. Many factors are evaluated to enact the requests for money. The pleas from those desiring objects are great. Think now of the world and helping others. This is why a person is brought to Earth. This is why you are here!

Can we communicate with angels who are overseeing another person?

Yes, it is accomplished as requested. Whoever is asked will come forth to receive messages. We are to bring wellness and compassion to souls. You can write to the angels. Your writing to angels is read and understood. Angels can help relations with others by guiding the souls to open their hearts to love.

We must let people decide their own destinies, but we can help if it is God's plan. If you feel that you cannot communicate with a particular soul, it is correct to ask to communicate with the angel overlooking this soul. The angels understand all ways in the lives of their charges. A person's angel can help to let the soul receive the message. This can be helpful in easing tensions and sending love. Many things can be helped in life by this communication.

Is a female's intuition or a man's gut feeling valid?

We whisper truths to the soul. It is up to the soul whether to listen or not listen. To be aware of angelic voices, you should be in the eternal soul, not in the body. A wonder of wonders may occur in the soul when, at times, a person can hear us or may feel our motion of vibrations. If a soul has an urge to perform an action, it may be a surge of prompting from surrounding angels. Listen to your soul. When this is ignored, errors may occur in life.

We only try to help you with your life, as we know all of the past and the future. The way to do this is to be in soul awareness and sustain a vibration of a higher, more-profound level of consciousness. Your life is you in your eternal soul, not your outer body. Know this.

Dealing with Anger

How do we get rid of anger?

When the body and mind are thankful, the mind can weld with the angels. Let go of anger. Let the angels help you. When you think of bad things that have happened to you, let go of each memory as it becomes a thought. Forgive the world. God in heaven holds the sorrows you've wrought about the world.

Forgive others, as you would expect God to forgive you. Let go, because the anger holds you to a low level. Lift to the higher levels of thought. As the thought brings feelings of anger, let the thought also bring the letting go of the anger. Meet the thought by welcoming new levels of the mind and forgiving while focusing on why the angels want you to let go of anger.

Angels touch your heart to weld feelings and emotion. We let no one hurt your heart more than is bearable. Touch your heart with your mind. Together they will make things right. We see into people's hearts. The love felt is so important. Nurture all the love from the heart. Expand the love and the gentleness. Feel the love. The heart lets the mind think about these feelings.

Nothing is hidden from the angels, because we see the real you and understand why you do the things not of your worth. We watch the people of Earth respecting acts of kindness. This is found in what is done and what is not done. This is found in helping others. We watch the souls trying to do right, trying to uplift humankind. God honors these people in his kingdom.

To give your own happiness for another is to love God. He is watching. We will not turn away from helping those who would suffer. We try to send love to the leaders of wars to help their souls evolve. We hold them in our hands to tell them love can end the suffering of all humankind.

Open the Soul to God

How can we feel our hearts?

Your lives are assigned for this life. You have sat with your angels and decided the best course of action for your growth. Small changes may be made, but you will adhere to the basic restrictions of your life. God will let the spirit soar to heaven after life is over.

You are a soul. When we speak of you, we speak of the enduring soul, not the physical body. The physical body is not you but an expression of your soul. In the human body, the physical and the soul can grow together in consciousness. It is a place where a soul can experience in a physiological way. The soul has a heart and a mind. It is more subtle than the physical, but it is the true self.

The most important words come from the soul's mind, because it exists for all time. The soul is to be nurtured as your true self. Listen to thoughts and feelings from your soul. Love is felt in the strongest intensity and given to God or to other beings. This is to be cherished. One who feels deeply is opening the heart to pain and to love. The deepest emotions live within the soul's heart.

Where the soul's heart is not able to penetrate, the mind knows no feeling. This gives no soul growth. Let the love in the deep soul pour out to all who can be affected by this intense love. This openness will help you to feel God.

When we speak of movement of the heart, the heart of which we speak is not the physical heart. It is the heart in the soul, which has feelings deeper than the mind can fathom. A plan of the heavens is movement on Earth. God in heaven will manifest all life on Earth. Each creation has a plan. Each living soul has a plan. The world has a plan. The plan is dictated by the one God, and it will be followed by all creatures. The desires of humankind are in accordance with God's plan.

Never Fear Angels

Should people be afraid of dying if they see an angel?

Angels are never to be feared. We are the holy angels of God and are a delight in the heavens. We know of many ways to help. We listen to prayers directed to God, the Father in heaven. He directs us on what action to take. We meet to discuss ways to answer prayers. The burden is great on us. We act in purposeful ways directed by God with full knowledge of the soul's past and future.

We do not err. We act as God's light on Earth. Lifting a soul to God at the end of its life is a great action. Souls may beg. If we are told, "Do not take this soul now," this is God's word. We cannot go against God's word. We will not go against God. The soul may be needed in another place. We will be with you in times of sadness, in times of joy and glory, or in times of reverence as we watch your solemn ways. Do not dismiss us from your presence, as we are real and are with you at all times.

A God in the heavens who will send his angels to be with a soul is a great God. Angels will hear your cries, touch you in order to bring comfort, and watch over you as a soul protector. Tell people to be ready to be of help to others; forget opulent living and help the many who will need much during this time.

Many have had experiences of someone coming out of nowhere appearing to help, then disappearing. Were these angels?

Yes, they were probably angels, who need not wear the clothing of heaven. They may appear as any person who has ever lived.

There are also spirits who have died violently and are not ready to enter heaven who may remember where they were most comfortable. They may stay on Earth for hundreds of years if they so desire. A soul who feels it is not deserving of heaven may need to remain here on Earth to understand before it lets the angels show it heaven. You may be able to see these spirits. Don't be afraid. These spirits have no power to enact change. They are unable to hurt anyone except by invoking fear.

How do we thank the angels for all their help?

When angels help their charges, we expect no thanks. The loving ways we give to the souls we oversee is our joy. The love exalts us. The more love we feel, the brighter our joy. We see and feel your thoughts. When anything wonderful happens in the world, we are witness to it. When people give to others who need these things, this is a wonder on Earth. We speak of food now, but it could be other things. People who give selfishly for the happiness of others are a joy to behold.

Angels receive all blessings these mentions behold. A grateful heart is seen and felt. This is honored in our ways. The heart with thankfulness is given the most honorable worth. This love is felt throughout the heavens. All love is felt by the angels. The worthy heart and soul will lift to be exalted by the angels. Go to the world and tell everyone that the angels give much to help the souls of Earth. Tell them we are with them in order to help them.

CHAPTER FOUR

Birth on Earth

You choose the moment of your birth: the day, the year, down to the moment that the light of creation enters the body. When the birthed one wants a new body from the heavens, he or she asks the angels to allow birth on Earth. If it is necessary for the soul's growth to enter the world, it is declared. You are born into the world of your own making by choosing a mother, the birth date, and the place of birth. When a soul enters the body, the child and mother are united. This merger lives beyond Earth. This is a merger of souls who knew each other before this life. Then the child is born unto Earth.

The soul of the child will move in and out of the mother's body during the carrying. It is in and out, but it will be permanent when the child is born. This is the time of birth. This is the second of birth. The soul enters the body at the moment of birth, and it leaves the body at the moment of death. All souls will enter heaven. We will be with every soul as it is born and as it returns to the heavens.

Coming into Life on Earth

What can you share about the moment of birth?

It is a profound experience to enter Earth. This is a wonderful occurrence: The soul existing within a physical body can now grow toward God by way of the senses. Life on Earth is a method of growing and feeling. When the soul can feel the growth of love with all its values and attributes, this can be a way to lift higher toward God. Life in a human body is an honor. It is a wonderful thing to be in a human body. To live ife on Earth is to be treasured, as this is a way to grow to God. The soul will grow in a human body.

Let all know that life on Earth is to be cherished. Do not diminish this life on Earth. Do not diminish the growth of the soul. One is not to end life before the natural ending of the body. Live all life and let this be as God deems on Earth. The movement of the soul will guide the decisions of life.

Why can't we remember the past?

One needs to know this life only. Before this life, the lessons were completed. All the moments have been conveyed to who you are now. This life, this moment, is all you need to be concerned with. Now is the important moment. Would you be hampered with the past? We will let glimpses occur in the mind if they are necessary for understanding a current or future occurrence. Let go of the past and be involved in the present.

God is now. God is the way to experience the fullness of everything. Experience life now as if it were your last moment on Earth. Share the love inside you with the world. Give all the love you can. The love you hold in your heart will be with you when you lift to heaven. When this love is full and complete in each person on Earth, what will you be feeling? What thoughts will you have? Will you be in fear or immersed in love and thankfulness?

We are with you every moment. We want to love with our thoughts and know each soul feels the love. Plan to live in your highest, finest thoughts. These precede the actions. You can affect the actions of the world.

You must let go of the past. Be here now, in this moment. God is here in all life. This is the life you have chosen. Live it with all the intent you can create.

Can we remember heaven after we are born on Earth?

Most worlds are only lowly manifestations of the heavens. When the soul enters heaven, the feelings of remembrance are overwhelming. The soul is ecstatic that it has returned to this wonderful joy. In this life on Earth, you have a yearning that can't be explained in this world. Can you make sense of something only felt and not reasoned? Some feel displacement in this world, as if they should be in another place. This is the soul's longing for heaven.

Some feel half in heaven and half on Earth. They are uncomfortable with life on Earth. This is a desire to be in heaven. When life begins, previous lives are not remembered by most minds. Needless to say, the new child begins this life as the new body is given. The soul may feel a faint remembrance of heavenly life. The soul is unable to identify this desire.

Live now, not in a past life or in a future life. This is the moment of concern. This is where you are meant to be now. You arranged this life with the angels before coming here. Experience every moment of life.

Is the soul at its full maturity when newly born on Earth? Is it the same at two days old as it is at age ninety?

No, the age of the person does not matter. The soul is of no age. The soul will grow toward God during life through a myriad of experiences, through thought and through the senses.

Experiences in life may bring one closer to God, not by sustaining peacefulness in the body but through experiences that you might not think would have any influence on the soul. The growth could happen in a moment or over many years of life. It could be a tremulous occurrence or an unmemorable movement.

The growth of the soul is why many souls return to Earth. The soul's wish is to be viewed favorably by God and all the gods in thought. A soul can grow in the body to varying degrees. Some may stay through many lifetimes. Others may only need birth on Earth to feel what it is like being in a human body and know it is not needed. All movements during life — all thought, all feelings, all action —are necessary to move closer to God. Hearing, sight, and touch are all used in the growth of the soul.

The love felt is most important, as God is all love and light. To feel even a part of this love on Earth will help bring a soul into the light of the heavens. Life on Earth desires to be lifted to the heavens. God sees the light of your soul. Every emotion, every conflict, every experience on Earth is a way of growing in the body.

Why are people born to specific families? How does ancestry fit into the picture?

Souls choose the families they are born into. As a child is born, it is given the ways of its parents and ancestors. When the most valuable traits are received through the genes, the person becomes part of that family.

The linage is given to the child. The traits of ancestors are given to the new soul. They knew you in the heavens and planned for you to enter the family linage. A soul knowing its ancestors is a most cherished child; the ways are passed to the new soul to reach God through the shelter of the family.

States of Bodily Health

Why are some people born with deformities or afflictions?

The people who are born on Earth with deformities were told of this before coming to Earth, and these were agreed on. The necessity of being born in a physical body is crucial to the development of the soul.

The soul may want a way to grow to God but feels the need to pay for ways of the past. These are not things punished by God. These are self-imposed punishments. You may feel the need to avenge or to purge past actions. Ask what you can do to make amends.

The angels suggest ways the soul can decide its own life and its life's adversities. Much can be done. The physical body is necessary for a specific way of growth at certain levels. The senses are to be used to develop feelings through a physiological method. This is not to say growth in all fields is done through a physical body, only on a particular field of growth. This begins as a soul is born in a body and ends with the release of the soul upon the death of the body.

Higher levels of growth need no physical body. All adversities or deformities, whether physical or mental, are carried out with complete understanding and acceptance by the soul. This is accepted and at times even requested for the purpose of what the soul feels is necessary for accelerated growth to God. In God's eyes, all are in perfection. The soul has no deformities.

If God doesn't feel deformities, illnesses, and afflictions are necessary, why do the souls or the angels let them happen?

We understand the question, but the power of the individual mind is very intense. If the soul feels strongly that it must make amends for a past action, the angels will discuss varied options with it. The soul then decides its life path.

Life here on Earth is so short compared to lives on other worlds or in the heavenly realm. The physical body on Earth is seen as of little importance as a vessel. The soul does not carry an affliction into eternity, but the soul may see a temporary affliction as a method of ridding itself of past errors. This cannot be explained in mortal terms, as the human mind cannot comprehend all the workings of God.

Deformities and afflictions are not to be looked on as incorrect, for we honor the requests of the soul if they are in accord with the soul's life plan. This is the correct action in God's eyes. Time is a factor in this answer.

Must we pay for our sins with a physical or mental affliction?

No, not at all. God is not punishing these souls. God welcomes all souls with open arms. The individual soul may feel an indebtedness and request a deformity or an illness in order to make amends. This may accelerate the path to God in the mind of the soul.

Many wish to rid the soul of all encumbrances and all that they perceive as sinful from their pasts. A human mind wants wonderment in life but realizes the wonders of the heavens far outshine limited mortal existence. In the heavens, plans are often made to go through earthly sufferings, so life in the heavens is in all perfection for all time.

Do the angels tell the soul this isn't necessary?

Yes, a conversation takes place in which it is explained. However, the soul's desires are given as requested. The soul may have performed horrific actions, and even though it's explained that nothing stands between it and God, the soul still feels it necessary to make amends. This really happens. This is true. Know this is not a life of permanence. It is a temporal condition.

What happens if this affliction is too hard a punishment? Can this be changed after birth?

Yes, all things may be discussed with your angels. When meetings are convened with a soul's angels and it is agreed that an affliction is too much for the soul to bear, it is then lifted, or the soul may decide to stay in a heavenly plane to rest.

Many angels will surround the soul to bring it to heaven. When the soul is made well, it is in ecstasy. Many lessons are learned by the soul. It remembers these when it is again in a body and uses judgment in its actions.

If the light of creation enters at the moment of birth, does this mean abortion is all right to perform?

Abortion is not a way of God, as it was declared the soul was to be given a body. The soul is not affected because it shall be born at a different time to another. Plans must be constructed again for the birth. The plans of the soul will be reworked for the birth to occur. This will be done.

The interrupted birth is not a wonderful occurrence, whether it is by abortion or by miscarriage. It is a sad event. This is not a murder of the child because life enters the womb at the moment of birth, but it is sad because a life will now be deterred to another time.

To abort the delivery of the child opens the soul of the mother to feel. This can open the heart to higher levels, but it is small consolation for keeping the child from being born. The soul of the mother needs fulfillment in her life path, as does the father. Some pains were planned and meant to be endured. It is important for others not to judge these decisions, for only the parents and their angels know all the reasons and repercussions of this action. Let all be as they are, for they are on their own path.

Plans Aren't Rigid

In regard to the preplanning of events before we come to Earth: Is there something more? Some events are spontaneous, aren't they?

Yes, there is spontaneity, and there are accidents, but all have been viewed prior to life. All possibilities are felt, but your life plan is selected according to what is needed in your growth to God. All incidents involve myriad factors, including thoughts, fears, actions, and external influences. All is seen: the past, the present, and the future. All synergize to form an event. All life and all feelings are known and discussed before being born on Earth.

A most wonderful life could have been requested, but many possibilities are open to change. The most perfected and planned life is susceptible to change by the fulfillment of desires during life. Events are subject to human will, to human thoughts, to the integration of each other, and to feelings of the heart.

All the gods and angels in the heavens contribute to the outcome of any action. The possibilities of any action can change reactions. Would one who loves another soul so greatly come into the world to save his or her great love from an accident, disfigurement, or death? All changes are not made from feeling. Circumstances foreseen from the heavens can bring wonderment to one or many. The changes can occur from the vision of the varied possibilities of life.

Repercussions of actions can reach beyond this lifetime. Possibilities of all events can be seen from the heavens. Some specifically request to give their lives for a cause or to help others in unknown ways. This is done as a prayer as one is ushered into the heavens. This tells of the goodness in the soul. This is a giving of oneself for others. This is not known on Earth. The soul is in glory as a soul of light and of brilliance.

So all is not preplanned, correct? Accidents can change life?

Yes, the born soul has a life plan to fulfill. The moment that changes a life through an accident or unseen circumstance was known by the soul before birth. This is not remembered during life. Souls may be viewed as having no age, so even though being hurt as a child may be viewed as a terrible event whereas an injury to elderly person is viewed as not so terrible, the soul does not age.

A deformity or a defect is asked for by the soul in order to lift itself to the higher heavens. The soul feels this will help pay for sins committed in other lives. This soul requests a way to pay for what it determines as sins. Many possibilities, many choices, many probabilities, and many outcomes are given during life. These come from wanting to live as happily as possible.

A moment of questioning comes from a moment we consider an error, but it may be part of one's life plan. Accidents can occur that were not preplanned but are instead reactions to a momentum of irregular events. This occurrence will not have been foreseen.

All lives are subjected to phenomena from varied levels and varied sources. All prepositioned plans are subject to alteration. As there are infinite possibilities, choices are given and secured by the soul. One may move as the soul moves, or one may fight against all preplanned goals. An experience that shocks the soul is not usually preplanned, because the soul is aware of all plans for life. Yes, these can occur. A life may be forever altered by a movement not of the soul's own making.

A disease or dysfunction gently accepted by the soul is often planned before birth. The reasons are known only by the soul and are only for this hurried life on Earth. People going to war may realize the maiming or death that may occur. Yet they go to war because their beliefs and feelings are stronger than the fear of disablement. This is much like life on Earth for a disabled person. When the soul decides to come to Earth, the body and mind are subject to earthly phenomena. The growth to be closer to God after this life is stronger than the fear of entering Earth.

Does disablement mean one can be closer to God? No. In the mind of the soul, however, this is a truth. The soul feels that it can live in a state other than wholeness to pay for its past sins. The soul offers life to God. It gives alms to God by the enactment of ridding itself of what it perceives as sin. The soul has seen the higher heavens and begs to be in them.

The soul knows many truths not unveiled to mortals. As people realize their souls and merge, their actions will become more in accordance with God. Lives on Earth are so fleeting. We ask you to merge with the higher ways during life. All ways to God shall be opened to you. Lift to meet him through purity of thought and through loving.

A lot of people will question your explanation of events being preplanned. Can you explain it in a different way?

Let the words stand as written. The complexities of the mind and soul are to be now known in the world, as these writings will declare. The complexities are given without mention to change preset phenomena.

Thought in the mind is susceptible to fluctuation, causing interruption of impending phenomena. One can try to bind the thought and action by strict adherence to a known system of rules, but the mind will rebel because the natural movement is freedom. When this freedom also holds spontaneity, it will grow. Binding to rules of conduct allows no movement of growth. On Earth, much frustration abides. Factors beyond mortal understanding enact the phenomena that occur.

The mind punishes itself through feelings of unworthiness for not living in the state of perfection. Many predetermined events happen because of this. Many occurrences happen due to thought prior to being born on Earth, but they are influenced by the workings of the thought in the mind at the second of the occurrence.

The world is not now in a state of grace or love. It is a many-troubled world. Freedom of thought must always have a flow. Thought must never be hampered. Feelings are never to be hampered. Discretion and care will always have influence in action. No one is to hinder the formation of human thought.

God is a feeling of more graciousness than can be comprehended by the human mind. The world now needs to administer care and discrimination to the performance of actions. The ways of physical performance must be deliberated before activity. The ways of humanity must now be altered to accommodate the growth to God. God will tolerate humanity's ignorance in eons of time. Humanity must change its behavioral patterns now in this age. A lifting of the soul, a communication with the angels, a devotion, and a thankfulness — all must be invoked.

The Soul's Purpose

Are some people born on Earth to achieve certain things?

Yes, these are planned as the soul is in the heavenly abode watching Earth. The soul plans its life with angels and celestial entities; many times the soul plans a specific act to perform on Earth before entering the body. A group of souls may plan particular significant acts to perform during life. They might plan to enter Earth in the same era in order to achieve this as a group action.

All souls think and act with complete free will. The mention of these group efforts is only a design of the life plan. This may or may not be in accordance with God's plan for the souls of Earth. A child of God may listen to the heavenly words or may disregard them. People may work toward God or against him, with God's plan or against it.

Are souls brought to Earth to commit specific acts?

If a person is murdered, the murder was planned before birth. When accidents happen, they were planned before the souls involved entered Earth. They were planned to let the soul experience some feelings that it must experience.

No man on Earth knows the reasons or the far-reaching repercussions of an act performed by either a soul or an angel. There is no way we could explain to mortals the reasons one would be sent to perform a horrific act. No one on Earth can understand the workings of the heavens.

If a soul is asked by an angel to perform a task such as this, it is necessary to know it is for an important reason and should not be questioned. Souls may be sent to Earth to perform requested acts of wonder as well.

This is a great honor. When one is asked by the holy angels of God to perform a task, it is usually a given that the souls of Earth do not have enough understanding of these acts to condemn them or question God's laws.

A soul may enter Earth in a state of purpose to commit a specific act. If someone is killed in an accident, this is preplanned. The soul was told before entering Earth. The soul causing the accident may have been brought here for this purpose. The soul can change its life path and do the opposite of God's will. When this occurs, the soul will then be ready to relive this, as God directs.

Are particular discoveries or inventions planned by God to occur at specific times on Earth?

Not in the way you think. God prepares the soul to achieve a specific action on Earth, but it may not achieve this in its life on Earth. Many discoveries and many creations are planned before entering life on Earth, and the soul may instinctively perform the action with the remembrance of this desire.

Many discoveries cannot be obtained at the time of the specific soul's life on Earth because of the low level of thought and energy in Earth's atmosphere. When this thought is perceived on Earth, several minds may realize the thought. This is in the atmosphere. This does not come directly from God. The souls planned the wonder from the wonders of the heavens before coming to Earth. All comes from God through the people's minds.

Did the souls also plan events and happenings on Earth, such as the Panama Canal, Lewis and Clark, world wars, and so forth?

Yes, the way to explain this is to tell you Earth is in constant movement. Changes must occur on Earth. This movement could be perceived as good or bad. All are conceived by the minds of souls in the heavens as they planned their lives on Earth. The world's incidents are generated by thought. Discoveries are generated by thought. All things of Earth are thought first and manifested into reality.

God has given this power to the souls of Earth. God has given each soul the power to enact its own life. Some people have lofty plans. Some people have none. Some people wish to be born in a specific place at a specific time to perform a specific act on Earth.

Why would anyone want to return to Earth?

If the soul desires to re-enter Earth, it may be born here again. We don't restrict the soul's desires. One may not want to return to Earth, as it is a lowly plane, but it can be done. This is a choice of the soul. We may help. The soul may decide another world may be more desirable, or it may remain in heaven. It is familiar with Earth and may want a body again. One of wisdom who wishes to teach and help others may re-enter Earth to do this.

Some long-sought, unfulfilled goals may be attempted again in a new life. Rest assured, the desire to be in a body again is strong, but not all souls are born again on Earth. Some are more comfortable as souls in heaven. Whatever is needed for the soul to grow to God will come to be.

Soul Groups

Do souls ever choose to be born on Earth at the same time?

Yes, souls may have a similar goal that they wish to accomplish on Earth. They may decide to be born in the same area or country at a similar time. They will meet in life to help attain this goal. Souls in the heavens know each other and discuss mutual goals and plans they would like to initiate on Earth. They ask the angels if this can be a part of their life plans when they are born on Earth. Many times this helps decide when the body is born. Souls can, if desired, meet on Earth to accomplish their group's plan.

We see the needs of those with deep love or purpose who wish to be together on Earth to accomplish a goal. They plan their births to do this, on Earth or on another place. If friends, relatives, or loved ones are together in heaven, they may ask to meet or know each other on Earth. This can be done. The souls are given ways to find each other by the angels. The ways are given and are arranged by the angels.

Can we change our destinies?

Choices were made to be welded with the mind. Once on Earth, a person is open to changing the predestined welding. Humans letting go of choices made before entering their bodies will not make this life as good as possible.

Before entering their bodies, humans see their lives as they could be with different possibilities. This could make life on Earth better by paving the way before entering into the body. The soul has the choice to create, mend ways, work toward helping humanity, or do what it knows are wrong actions. It is the soul's decision only. These are tests the soul wishes to attempt before it enters the body. When it passes these tests, the soul may elevate toward God.

What tests?

Not all of the words are meant to change life plans before coming to Earth. The soul may request tests in the opening to lift closer to God. These tests are meant to show the character of the soul. The tests can show the soul's worth and merits if these were not shown in life on Earth. Life plans can be altered, but this may deter the souls from the easiest way to God.

CHAPTER FIVE

Preparation for Death

How does a person get over the death of a loved one?

This is something we angels do as a mention. The angels know the pain of a person's heart. We surround the soul of that person and send thoughts of calm and solace. If the soul is aware of our presence, it is calmed and protected.

Understanding the progression of the soul after death may help. The person must go through the grief of the separation. The love of the departed soul is important for the movement of feelings within the soul.

Knowledge of the eternal may help the pain. The soul is an eternal being that does not end with the death of the body. Try to think of the future to make life fulfilled without the physical body of the loved one. Know you will see your loved one again. You will be with him or her again. Be strong. Be your most courageous self. You can get through the pain with help from the angels.

The departed soul's appearance in the opening of the heavens will help it assimilate the changes. Let the soul go to the heavens. Let the angels surround you and help you with your pain. If the feelings of helplessness and pain hurt more than is bearable, ask God for solace to help you through the most painful moments. Feel the angels, as they are truly with you at this time sending thoughts of calm and love. Write to your loved ones who have departed. This will help them in lifting and help you in your sorrow.

Life Goes On

What can you tell people preparing to die?

When the body is readying for death, let it know this life on Earth is not the whole existence. Life goes on into eternity. *The person that is you will always be you. More wonderful experiences than you can ever imagine are ahead of you.* Life beyond this life is eternal and forever, becoming more and more real with every birth and death. The needs of love are the same in the heavens as on Earth. When souls enter heaven, the emotions are with them. The moments so treasured on Earth will be felt in the heavens.

When loved ones lift to the heavens, they are getting ready to be united with you at another time. You will be free to love. The heavens are so lovely. It will be joyous to go there. All who die in the body will be lifted to see all the heavens. We don't want people to think they will reside in another place.

When the end of your life comes, let yourself know you've lived. Now wait only to weld with the angels. When you know you have awaited death not with wasted hours but with loving thoughts, you have a good life.

When the end of life comes and you await only your meeting with angels, it is a peaceful, gentle death. When your thought remembers only why the love is still in your heart, the goodbyes are for a world past and moments gone. All can see the wonders of heaven. When the soul readies to leave the body, it trembles and moves. When the heart opens to see the heavens, angels appear to lift the soul. Death is a lifting, nothing more.

When the spirit leaves the body, God is present. He will watch the lifting and the wonder. When the spirit lifts out of the body, the body withers but the spirit soars into joy. The wise know it well from remembrance. You are lifted into bliss and the glory of God. You are with your loved ones who have gone before.

The lifting of souls into heaven is not to be feared. This is a lifting to what the soul most desires. The feelings of bliss ascend with the soul. They are multiplied as the soul lifts to higher levels of heaven.

Arriving in Heaven

Many souls will enter heaven at the death of the physical body. This is a lifting of the soul accompanied by angels. We meet the souls and lead them to a place where they are prepared to meet God. You may see all levels of heaven, and you will understand all things again. You will love the transition you are shown. An angel will show you your life on Earth to let you comprehend your future choices. May the lifting reveal many truths to the soul.

You may wait if you are afraid to watch your past life on Earth. If you are not afraid, you will meet the angels to plan your will, plan your next life in God's universes. The waiting may be for a long time if that is what you want.

Not one person has sinned who cannot see heaven. God has love for all. When heaven is entered, angels are lifted to God. This is the greatest experience one can ever know. The day of lifting is wonderful for the soul. It is a day many should cherish. This day is made clear to the soul before coming to Earth.

There is a powerful beginning and ending to human life. What is referred to as death is a much-desired beginning to the real life ahead. A sorrowful and fearful end of this life on Earth is not a weakness. It is a real feeling of those not prepared for death. When giving beginnings and endings to the world's bodies, God works the natural movements of the soul into change. These life endings are only a passage of your mortal bodies to renew into light and love.

When your soul lifts to the heavens, you are aware of rising from the body. You are aware of death. We help soothe the fears by surrounding the soul with welcoming arms. It is a pleasure to experience, leaving the body. Thought goes on forever. Last thoughts and words are for this world. When the body has been left behind, the soul still thinks and speaks. When love is felt at the end of life, it does not cease. It is felt even more deeply.

Your True Self

You are you now, and after death, you will have no pretense, no angers, and no sadness. You will be the truest individual you can experience. When the true, natural you begins life in the heavens, love surrounds you. We need the words to tell you in language you can follow. When the body dies, the soul lifts up to be one with God. The soul lifts in ways to give you both Earth and the heavens.

What will you feel when the end of your life comes? We think forgiveness for errors made, closeness to family, true feelings known, and a heart full of love and compassion would be most wanted. Knowing you helped others and have done the best you could to ease pain in the world would be wanted. Measure yourself by your own standards and sense of values. While you will err greatly in the world, try to be the best you can experience.

Planning Life on Earth

Is there a time to be born and a time to die?

The moment of birth is ordained in the heavens, and the moment of death is contracted before birth. The moment of death will not be remembered within the human life.

You can postpone death by prayer to God or by healing from the angels surrounding you. Circumstances may change to prolong your life or change the path of your life. This is all made clear to your soul.

The scientific workings of the movements of force inhibit the effects concerning the span of life. The moment of death may be deterred by the actions of heavenly beings. There is a basic plan for each life. In almost every circumstance, it is enacted. This plan may be changed, however, as all laws on Earth are subject to change.

God can enact changes at any time. Angels can work miracles to extend life on Earth. Blessings and healings can help the body in miraculous ways. Prayers to help the body can help free the soul for an easy lifting, and they can help the body calm and create a peaceful atmosphere for the body and mind to coordinate to move the soul.

Prayer will give the soul comfort to prepare for lifting. It surrounds the soul for passage, making the soul lighter for movement. Fear subsides in the mind. Love and prayer for the dying do all these things.

Is life predestined?

Physical ailments are predestined because they are agreed on before coming to Earth. The life you have is not completely predestined. People have choices, and they will often choose erroneously. Angels will try to help, but often wrong decisions are made.

The basic life path is predetermined. The most important decisions are made before coming to Earth, but at times, they are not remembered by the soul. Your life was told to you by the angels before you entered the realm of Earth. You agreed to it. God planned it for you to experience the feelings you need for growth into new worlds. Your life is planned by your past actions before you entered the world. A changed life order will be fulfilled at another time.

The purpose of the soul on Earth is to lift to God in a way that cannot be allowed without a physical body. When your soul is in a body, it can experience growth through the senses. This can only happen in a body.

Your lives are reassigned for this life. You have sat with your angels and decided the best course of action for your growth. Small changes may be made, but the basic restrictions of your life will be adhered to. God will let a spirit soar to heaven after its life is ordered.

How does the soul know when it wants to reenter Earth?

We give you great gifts. Your heart will be lifted to a place in God's love. We will give you words to give to everyone. We are now sending forth the words.

When we make plans to begin a new life or end a life, we ask the soul to let us know what it wants. The soul tells us when it is time to begin its new life. Sometimes the person is not even consciously aware of this communication. The soul, in its purity, tells us its life will now change into a new birth.

Sometimes it is planned before you come to this Earth. Other times, it is determined after you begin this life. One is usually not conscious of this arrangement with the celestial beings.

Souls on Earth

As many lift at the death of the body, what happens to those who don't?

Some souls will reside on Earth in spirit until it is time to lift to the heavens. The Mallbon angels determine when the soul is lifted. A body may have died but the soul refuses to lift to God, or the soul might still be filled with fear of the unknown and afraid to lift from Earth. If the soul died in a horrific way, you need to absorb this and process this in the mind of your soul.

Generally, this processing is done in the opening of the heavens, but some may decide to stay with what is known to assimilate the painful memories. The pain and fear is usually what keeps souls earthbound, but deep love can also hold you to Earth. A soul may want to stay with a loved one until his or her death. You are not aware that you can see the loved one from heaven, so you remain near him or her and try to communicate.

The more the soul is freed from ignorance, the easier the lifting. If you are afraid you will go to a burning hellfire, you will not leave Earth, and you will wander in spirit so as not to be punished for what you perceive as sin. This is regrettable.

Are all welcome in heaven? What about the cruelest, most horrible, evil people, such as mass murderers?

Yes, all are welcomed to the heavens. The people of whom you speak are welcomed in the lowest level of the heavens. Those souls may wish to change the manner they have lived and grow to God.

They are punished only by their own thoughts. They know the thoughts and feelings of everyone they have hurt in any way. This weighs heavily on them. They beg for mercy. Life in this heaven is merciful.

These souls will go to a place of repose and contemplation. If they are heavy with the weight of past decisions or evil actions, the most lowly heaven will give them a place to consider their past behavior. They can see the higher heavens and may want to repent these sins to lift to a higher place.

These souls are given sight of God's heavens but have much to reflect on. They may return to the opening of the heavens to talk with the Men of Decision, or they may reside in the most lowly heaven.

They will find happiness there and a much-needed peacefulness. They know now of the glories of the heavens and can feel some of the joys, even in the lowest of God's heavens.

When such a soul is ready to view the life it lived on Earth, it requests this. It may need consoling from the angels. The soul knows of all harm it has caused. This is viewed through thoughtful and compassionate reflection, as the lifting revealed many truths and understandings to the soul. It is no longer in ignorance.

After this viewing, the soul will feel remorse for past actions. A soul may request to be given birth again to make amends. It may be a long time before the terrors of its previous life can be assimilated by the soul's mind and heart.

A soul in this lowly heaven may give thanks for the merciful welcome of God and his angels. The soul is the same individual as it was on Earth but now has forgiveness, compassion, and understanding. This soul now views past actions from a different perspective and is aware of the pain it has caused.

Fear of Death

What can you share with those who are afraid of death?

Death is not to be feared as a part of life. We arrange the reunion of the loved ones in heaven and prepare the soul for the words from God. This is a welcome from the angels.

Once the word is received, the soul is allowed to play in the heavens. A wonderful joyousness falls over the soul as it rejoices in love. The wonder of heaven is bliss. No soul should be afraid to enter heaven.

The fear of death is only real if the ignorance persists. If the mind knows the glories awaiting it, it will cherish not only its moments on Earth but have expectations of wonderment for the lifting into blissfulness.

The death experience is a moment of culmination of wonderment. Imagine flying and being able to see all things and know all things. Shedding the mortal body sets the soul free to be its perfect self. All desires are fulfilled. All wonders are experienced. The ways of the heavens are known, and the life on Earth is shed.

What can you share with those who fear going to hell?

This is not for you or others. Do not be afraid because you think yourself not good enough to enter heaven. Even the most sinful of souls have a place in God's plan. A place will be waiting for all souls where each will find happiness.

We welcome every soul in the heavens. Just as in different parts of your life, you may have varied beliefs. The truth of all things is understood after the death of the physical body occurs.

These understandings lift the soul to a higher level. Vengeance is not for humanity to administer. No person knows the soul of another. Yet people perform sinful actions on Earth because they know no better. They are welcomed to heaven, just as the most holy of souls.

A man of work and toil is honored after death. He is elevated to the most high. A lady of leisure is given a place as well. We don't choose one soul over another. The soul will go where it is most comfortable.

Your view of the worth of people is distorted. A beggar on Earth might be a king in heaven. A rich person on Earth may be a student in heaven. No one should judge another because you don't understand others' souls and hearts. When souls lift to heaven, the angels sing. The wait to see the master is a reality.

What happens if someone is afraid to leave the body at the time of death?

We are waiting to tell you the way to meet the angels when you lift to heaven. You are to lift your love to meet God. This is a natural occurrence. When the angels come to lift you, the way to greet them is to be ready to lift with them. Try not to fight because you do not want to leave the body.

The fear of death is in many people of Earth. This will disappear as you are lifted closer to God. All understanding is entertained in the mind. The soul reaches more and more joy as it is lifted.

People of Earth may fear going to hell after death, so when it is time to lift to the heavens, they are afraid and fight with the angels coming to welcome them. Be not afraid, because each soul will lift to seek heaven. All souls are welcomed into the levels of the heavens. There is nothing to fear.

A person may fight God and wish to be in another place instead of God's abode. This will be discussed with the Men of One. This may be achieved only after many refusals of the paths of God and many lives following other than God. It is not a desired path as there is no joy. Most fear this path.

This will be discussed with the soul after all ways to reach God have failed. The many who are lifted should welcome the lifting. Know a chapter of your eternal life has ended, and begin your true life in the heavens or in other worlds, if that is desired.

All a soul has ever desired is in the true life ahead. All souls entering the heavens are awed by its magnificence. All souls are questioning, but comfort will be felt as they are lifted to meet their loved ones. Love binds all souls together. As loves are visited, ecstasy is felt in the soul.

The restlessness felt in life on Earth will be replaced by a peacefulness and joyousness. Don't be afraid to leave the body. The weak and fearful may not want to leave the body. Don't worry about those left behind on Earth. All will be well. The time to lift is ordained by God, who knows the reasons for every action. Your life on Earth had purposes. These were fulfilled as ordained. Go with the angels without fear. They only bring you into joy. The strong may fight the angels and demand to stay in the body. The body breathes no more. Let go and lift to God.

When an ordinary life is analyzed, it may seem nothing of importance was achieved. This may be viewed from another perspective. That life may have been for another reason than is visible from a mortal view.

The most seemingly insignificant life on Earth, when viewed by a mortal, appears not worthy of the slightest regard. But not all things of this soul are revealed to the humans around it.

The reasons of the heavenly angels or the gods are not to be judged. One on Earth has enough concern with becoming a higher soul, not with judging another's life. One day, all will be made clear.

After Life

What can you share about the moment of death?

The movement of the soul leaving the body is a trembling. It will be felt as a slight pull to heavens, as if one were breaking a thin veil. A most gentle movement is felt as the soul lifts toward the warmth of the angel's hand.

The angel, in the most tenderness one can feel, immerses the soul into the light of God's love. This is a sacred and complete surrender to God and the holy angels of all you have been in this life. The fullness of the heart overflows with emotion in the split second of the separation from the body. This instant is a complete giving of the soul to God.

Do we lose our personalities when we die?

There will be no change of personality in the change to heaven. You are and will always be you. A happier, more joyful you will emerge but with no loss of individuality. You will always be. When God holds you and gives you words, your soul will elevate to ecstasy. The true soul's desires are heard when a soul shows love instead of selfishness. A wonderment is born.

The life of a heavenly angel is forever. We are the never-ending followers of God and join with God in love. Your love and your life will go on forever. Don't worry about what is after this life. You will be cradled in God's arms.

What identifies the end of life?

When the years change the soul through new experiences, life will reach a point designated as the end. The time is preset by the planned one word. The life path is agreed on by the soul and the soul's angels. Only in specific instances is this life prolonged.

The end of life comes at a time when the purposes are fulfilled in that life. The soul may be needed in another place. The soul's growth may be completed in this particular life.

The life plan might be corrupted by wrong choices and the soul might want to redo the life or lift to the heavens to recompose a new life in a body. The life's end is preset but can be adapted by God or God's angels. The end of life on Earth is but a new beginning of the true life ahead.

What can you share about people who are in sadness when the end of their lives come?

When the sad enter heaven, the angels stay around to make sure their souls are comfortable and joyous. A guardian angel is with each soul of the world and rejoices when the charge lifts to a higher heaven.

Some souls who have little or no growth during life, who feel their dreams unfulfilled, or who have gone through long illnesses of the mind or the body, may be in depression or sadness even after the lifting into joy.

We stay with them and let them slowly adapt to all transitions. Their minds are given solace and peace until they can accept the wonders of the opening of the heavens. Their lives on Earth may have had no joy, and this is remembered. These souls are permeated with love and understanding of all things of the past.

If a soul ended its life with a sad heart, this sadness will not be sustained in the heavens. The soul will lift into blissfulness.

Are last rites important to give before the death of the body?

The movements and words of people of God giving last rites over a dying person are a prayer from compassion in the mind of humanity. The words are to prepare one for the lifting to the heavens.

These prayers are not necessary to lift to God because the opening of the heavens provides all the help for the soul needs. Prayer to help the lifting is a wonderful occurrence at the death of the body. Blessings and prayers are loving tributes to the dying.

Angels surround souls in comfort and love as they are lifted to the heavens. Love and prayers felt in the heart are received by the souls of the dying. This is all that is needed.

What is it like to die of old age?

It is the same is for humans as it is for animals. As the brain narrows, the mind begins a dream state. People may see themselves walking in a narrow tunnel, or they may see themselves floating on a ship. This is a tightening of the arteries in the brain.

This is a peaceful, soft death, as it is like being in a dream but awakening to meet the angels. This is falling asleep and awakening into bliss. This is a lovely way to leave the body.

Are souls approached by both angels of God and the devil after death?

No, the angels of God will come to lift the soul to its place in the heavens. Only if the soul begs during its life to meet the devil and abide in his realm of hell will the god of darkness appear at the time of death.

The decision will be made during the lifting to the heavens. At the opening of the heavens, if the soul requests to descend into hell, this is given. Until then, the angels of God protect the soul in all ways.

CHAPTER SIX

The Death of Children

Why do babies and little children have to die before they have even lived?

When the soul remembers heaven and longs to return, the cries are heard in the universe. Not all children can adapt to this life on Earth. Many a loved child may yearn in their souls for the arms of the Lord.

They will wait until the angels allow them to return. This is a mighty world to enter. It is a world of turmoil. Life is planned for each soul; if one is taken, the Father in heaven knows the reason.

Tell the parents that their child is one with God. One day they will see the child again and be with him or her in heaven. Many times a child is born on Earth who is more comfortable in heaven. The love from the parents may be deep and true, but the child cannot feel the blissfulness of the heavens and longs to feel this bliss. When this occurs, the soul of the child cries out to return. When the soul begs, we angels want to help. Even if the father and mother love the child deeply, it may be time to leave Earth.

How can we wait to lift these children until they are grown when all they need is to come to Earth? Souls may only need to come to Earth briefly to know it is not necessary for their growth.

Children Who Are Needed Elsewhere

Children who leave soon after coming to Earth are brought to God, who receives them as innocent. Your baptism rituals are not necessary to enter heaven. We welcome all souls to heaven. No one is omitted from God's love.

Children sometimes come to Earth to experience being in human bodies. They have memories of heaven and beg to return. If it is agreed they are to return, they enter the heavenly abode.

We lift the souls of those not needed on Earth. They may be needed in another place. You are not to judge the workings of the forces of God. All things happen for a reason. The child is needed in another place. The most important welding of the soul may be the welding that the child and the angels have experienced. All things are meant to happen as they will by God in heaven and the desires of the souls.

Children in Heaven

When a young child dies, how is that child treated in heaven?
When a new child is brought to the heavens, it is:

- first, lifted by the angels;
- second, brought to be with God; and
- third, lifted into the wonders of all heavenly beings
  to receive welcomes.

A child lifted to God is so pure that the growth it needed to fulfill on Earth has been accomplished.

If the loved ones on Earth could see and feel the love and wonders in the journey of the child, they would be in joy at its lifting. If only they knew what glorious wonders awaited the child, they would no longer be in pain over their loss. The purity of the child brings it to God directly. The love will now be made clear to all who knew the child. The love felt will lift the soul into higher levels in the heavens.

This is a wonderful experience. The loss of a child must be understood. This is not the joy lost on Earth but the joy given in the heavens. The child is needed elsewhere and the taking of the child has been weighed carefully. When this is known, the pain is not as deeply felt.

If you lose a child, it is imperative that you know not to hold blame or remorse in your heart. Let the child lift with love and thankfulness for the moments you spent with it. All souls must lift to the heavens at the time set by God. A wise person will realize this and surrender their love, knowing all souls will be reunited in the heavens.

When a child leaves Earth to return to heaven, it will remember life on Earth and send love to its family here. The child is happier there but will always remember every second of its life on Earth.

God will bless those who have lost their children. God will give them heavenly families to cherish.

Abortion

What happens to the soul if the child has been aborted by the mother?

The child to be born will return to a blissful heaven. It will be born at another time in the family. The child may not be born to the same person but may be a niece, nephew, or a grandchild.

Many children return to the heavens. This is a melting of emotions the soul must endure. We speak now of the parents and the child.

When a life is terminated, the soul of the child is richer for the experience. The child will find another way to enter Earth if this is its plan. There should be no guilt, as the child is in bliss.

Author's Note: When loved ones pass away, you tend to picture them as they were. You recall conversations of little importance you had with them.

A moment comes in the remembrance when you ask why couldn't you really connect with them? Why couldn't you really take a long look at them, really touch their souls, or really speak to one another with your hearts?

To do this would have opened your sheltered heart to pain, to suffering, to feelings. Perhaps the thought of it would be too painful, so you skim the surface of those moments. It's easier not to make the connection, to speak of nonsensical, Earthly things. However, to enter the most sacred, quiet chamber of the soul and share this with another, to speak soul to soul and really listen while the other soul answers, and to really feel what the other's heart is feeling takes more courage than most humans can employ.

CHAPTER SEVEN

The Lifting

What is a soul's understanding during the lifting?

A lifetime of worldly occurrences are viewed and seen as all other eyes have viewed them. All feelings are remembered. The feelings of others are made clear with understandings not known on Earth.

The soul is now made to understand all feelings, and with this knowledge, it perceives its future actions. When pain is experienced, it is remembered. People who made others suffer will know of the pain and suffering given to others. People who have given joy or peace will know the love from the people they have helped.

When a soul has loved another deeply, all the love is felt and understood, and all the pain of separation is felt and understood.

The mistakes one makes on Earth are viewed and seen without guilt, pain, or fear. It becomes a loving look at the past. Wrongs are viewed as past errors but made more meaningful by emotion. All is seen with understanding. The mind's thoughts can be read and feelings can be known when viewing one's life on Earth.

All truths are revealed to all souls entering heaven. These truths are not told to them. They are in the mind of each soul as it enters. All understanding comes to you. All knowledge is given to all who ask. The mind receives all knowledge from the heavenly wisdom all around.

We wish to tell you the soul feels bliss according to the nature of the hearts in humanity. A person may grow immensely in one second or may not grow at all for years. The level of the soul's growth determines the joy felt after the death of the body. Of all the pleasures in heaven, the lifting into joy is the most wanted.

This happens a moment after the soul leaves the body. There is wonder and an intense feeling of freedom of the soul. It is a joy unimaginable to lift with the angels. The soul is filled with questions and wants to talk with the angels. The angels lift the soul in a blanket of comfort and immense love. This is a most beautiful lifting.

Ascending into Your Real Life

How does the actual lifting feel?

The real life is not this life. The real life is your next life. During the lifting, there is no fear of letting go due to a lack of understanding about what will happen. Some on Earth feel all life will cease to exist. This is not true. All life opens before you during the lifting. When the soul comes close to feeling this, it is so slight that the soul can reach toward God or may return to the physical body. In a split second on Earth, this decision is made. It is a gentle pull toward God that takes a split second. The soul always lifts toward God, toward bliss, toward happiness.

This movement is a pulling out of the body to lift into blissfulness. There is a separation so faint, so subtle, that it is almost indistinguishable. A child may lift more readily than an adult because the heavens are still remembered. There is no desire to return to Earth as there is in an adult. Adults often see life on Earth as their only reality. They do not want to lose their lives because those lives seem to be everything they have. The more the soul is godlike, the more quickly it is lifted to the heavens. Souls will not tarry on Earth.

Do not ever fear the death of the body. The body you will have in the heavens is not physical as it is on Earth. It is a perfect soul illumination with the same thoughts, feelings, and desires you experience now.

You are all perfection filled with the light of God. You are the most perfect you that exists. You are any age or no age. You will be seen by others in a physical body.

The moment of the end of life on Earth is the moment of glimpsing the blissfulness of the heavens. The wonders of the heavens are more sacred, more lovely, and more joyful than can even be imagined by any soul on Earth.

This is the choice of the soul at the final second of life on Earth. The body shelters the soul from experiencing extreme feelings. The moment at the end of life on Earth is the moment of glimpsing the blissfulness of the heavens.

How will we understand the feelings of others?

The rising from the body will reveal all that is questioned. An understanding of the thoughts and feelings of any souls encountered during the previous life can be brought forth. All is known. The soul will understand all feelings, and all knowledge one may desire is revealed. Realize that this understanding is not received by the soul as a mortal mind but as a heavenly entity. There is a great difference.

Suicide

Is the soul still lifted if it commits suicide?

When humans give up the body by suicide, they are not having thoughts about what happens after they leave the body. The body dies and the soul stays on Earth in the same state of emotion it had a few moments before death. It can see and hear but cannot affect people or things of Earth. There is much more sorrow felt by them.

When the time comes for people to choose heaven, the angels lift them to see heaven. They will be taken to the level of heaven they need in order to weld with more joyful souls. They will be happy there.

When a body dies naturally, the soul is lifted. It will not wait to enter heaven. Only those who choose to remain on Earth will enter heaven when they are ready. When you are in heaven, you will want to see what remains on Earth. This can be seen. When you want to see those on lower levels of heaven, they can also be seen.

The soul will have a choice to lift to see heaven or stay with Earth. It is good to plan for a time. It is the choice of the soul. When in heaven, the soul can visit Earth to see its family and loved ones. The soul will be happy to try to communicate with them.

Life on Earth may end in many ways. God wants the soul to re-enter the heavens. When God leaves the methods of death to people, they may choose ways of killing not ordained by God. People may choose ways of accomplishing predestined events, but the results will be the same.

You almost want to leave Earth to enter heaven when you become aware of the wonderment of it, but you have to wait until the angels come for you. You may wait a few hours or many years. When you die naturally, you are lifted right away. If it is an accident, it is still pre-planned. If you take your own life, you may wait a long time before lifting to the heavens.

Author's Note: *Death is not a bad thing! Death is not something to be feared. I am not making light of losing someone you love. The shock and mourning are natural responses to losing a loved one.*

You'll do strange things in your numbness. You'll go through your cupboards trying to find something to feed the family who has come to be with you. You'll try to focus on their conversations: Why are they talking about politics? Don't they know why they're here? You really need to be alone. You wish everyone would leave you alone so you can smell your loved one's shirt and quietly remember those arms around you, recalling his or her voice.

Then it hits you that you will now be alone. How will you go on? Your mind goes into a rewind mode. Why wasn't I nicer? Why didn't I cherish every moment with my love? Why my loved one? Of all the people who could have died, why did it have to be my loved one? I didn't get a chance to say "I love you" before his or her death.

How can life be so fragile? How can you be here one minute and gone the next? Whirlwinds of thoughts surround you, overwhelm you.

The angels ask that you look at this life as only a small portion of the eternal life. Love remains forever. Life goes on forever. You will see your loved one again someday. You will experience all the feelings again, all the love again. Your loved one knows your thoughts and your feelings.

Death, in perspective, is a wonderful thing. Try to look at the larger picture, not just from your loss or from the perspective of Earth. This is not to make light of life on Earth, as every moment is so important. Right now, you don't think you will ever function again but you will. You will get through this! Pull the strength from within yourself, and feel your angels surrounding you and bringing peace to you.

CHAPTER EIGHT

Entering into the Heavens

Can you describe the area the soul enters when first lifting to heaven?

This is called the opening. This is the place where the soul restores and becomes comfortable with the lifting. The way is a path filled with love from the angels. This is a place to understand the death of the body and that the past life is now done. This is a glorious place that will put the soul at ease.

The angels will talk with the soul and will send much love. The soul will be calmed and will ready to lift to meet God. If the soul desires to understand anything from its past life, these things are shown to the soul until they are completely understood in all ways.

The heavens can be seen from the opening. This is an area where the soul is ready to meet God and lift to the heavens. This is to simulate feelings from the last life and understand the transition.

This will be a welcome wonder for the soul. The soul may view the life it lived on Earth until all understanding is evident. The Men of Decision help in any way possible to communicate with souls left behind on Earth. When the soul is comfortable with the transition into the heavens, the angels surround it and guide it into the heavens.

What else is given in this understanding? The fears of all souls entering heaven are revealed, as are all truths. These are in the minds of all souls as they enter. All understanding comes to them. This knowledge is in all minds wanting to know these truths — all knowledge from the heavenly wisdom all around.

A soul will feel past emotions and want to make amends for the hurts it has caused. If requested, this may be done if the ways of the gods decide it is necessary. The gods know not only each soul's growth but also the growth of all universes and all worlds. The souls are only involved with themselves, not others. When they begin to view how their lives can help others in the world, they take the first move toward being souls of love.

You have the wisdom of all things and complete understanding of all feelings in your entire life on Earth. You know why you felt certain ways and why others felt certain ways about you. The wonder of this is that you are full of love and compassion when viewing your life on Earth.

When you see the ways to progress to God, choices may change. You are not to be too concerned with finding a true love, because finding this love is now possible on Earth and in the heavens. In the heavens, this love will be found by the individual's soul, not as a sexual flirtation as it happens on Earth.

You see your life on Earth and know why all things happened. All is completely clear to you. You may watch with slowness to feel and understand each emotion, or you may will that the life be scanned quickly. An understanding of everything is known. This is a clearing of the emotions that are no longer needed in the soul. You know not only of every conversation but every thought and feeling others had toward you. You feel any love others had for you, and it feels wonderful to relive this.

Can those in the lowest heaven ever change their minds and go to hell instead?

The dark forces are never in the heavens. There exists no pull to tempt souls to hell. The souls in the lowest heaven have the choice, at the moment of death, to lift to the heavens or to go the way of the dark forces.

They remain in the heavens. Something inside them, in that instant, wants to be better and lift to God. In the split second of feeling heaven, this is done. The journey to God begins.

Past Lives

Is the opening the place where souls view their past lives?

Yes, if souls desire to understand anything from their past lives, these things are shown and completely understood in all ways. The Men of Decision are there to answer questions and help the soul understand anything necessary. The Men of Decision help the angels by taking the soul through all understanding of all things necessary to free the mind to pass into the heavens. They help the souls decide what is best for them to reach God.

The heavens can be seen from the opening. This is an area to ready to meet God and lift to the heavens. This is the time to assimilate feelings from the past and understand the transition. The souls are prepared and adorned with clothing they deem respectful to wear to meet God.

All this will be a welcome wonder for the souls. They may view the lives they lived on Earth until all understanding is evident. The Men of Decision help in any way possible to communicate with souls left behind on Earth and finish actions undone. When a soul is comfortable with the transition to the heavens, the angels surround the soul and guide it to meet God and lift further into the heavens.

Can souls view all their past lives there?

Yes, if there are any past lives, they can be understood in their entirety. The soul knows the true self. The soul knows all feelings, all knowledge from which has gone before.

This is a better way to make future goals for the soul. This may be a most interesting insight for the soul. Future decisions may be formed from a viewpoint of the growth of all lives. One can evaluate what is needed by the soul to grow toward God in order to plan future lives on Earth or in the heavens.

The soul will understand all feelings, all emotions, all ways needed to lift toward God. This is a time of repose and evaluation. Much understanding will be revealed to the soul.

Contact with Loved Ones

How do we — people on Earth — communicate with those who have died?

When a person of Earth wants to communicate with one who has left Earth, ask your angels to give them a message. This will be done. Another way is to write the feelings on paper. The angels will read it and know your feelings are true. They will understand your feelings and read your thoughts. Feelings are of the soul. This is pure and real in the soul. If you have feelings not expressed while your loved ones were on Earth, writing is the way to let your loved ones know your feelings.

These souls may need to understand your feelings in order to move on to their places in the heavens. All feelings should be expressed to those who have left Earth. This is a necessary communication. Every soul needs closure from its experiences on Earth.

Let the soul go into the heavens. If forgiveness is necessary, forgive the person and send the love in your mind and heart. If the person needs to forgive you, write to him or her asking for forgiveness. Bless the soul, send your love, and let the soul lift to the higher heavens. When this communication has been completed, it is a freeing of not only the person deceased but yourself as well.

What determines if what is written will be read by an angel or by the departed souls?

The words will be read by angels surrounding you. This will be done. If a soul wishes to read the words, this can also be done — either from the heavens or from behind you as you write.

People think all words must be said before the moment of death. This is not true. Think the strong thoughts or write the words you want the departed soul to know. You will understand after the death of the body.

We tell you that the words you give the one who has lifted should be given great worth. The words will be given, and the soul will remember these words into the heavens.

Ask the angels surrounding you to give these words to the soul. This will be given as requested. If you can feel the words' meaning — be it forgiveness, love, compassion, or empathy — the feelings will be conveyed. The feelings are true and unveiled to the soul. No masked emotions will be received. Your loved one in heaven will feel exactly what you feel.

Unfinished Business

Do unfinished works keep souls on Earth after death?

Yes, they sometimes wait until the pain of their loss is gone before lifting to the opening of the heavens. If the soul is made to know all the workings of the heavens, nothing will be left to understand.

At the moment after the death of the body, when the soul feels something is not done or that its leaving is more than those left on Earth can bear, it will ask the angels if the lifting can be delayed. The soul will ask them to wait until it comprehends the action of death. At the opening of the heavens, when the soul confers with the Men of Decision, it can request to see or hear its loved ones on Earth. This is usually granted, either by the soul coming to the Earth in spirit to watch or to communicate in another way.

The soul can watch and hear without returning to Earth. A decision is made about to the best way to communicate. This can be done from the heavens as well. The soul may feel something has not been clarified or finished, and this can be an emotional issue or another pattern of viewing a situation in its life. This can be a question that needs to be answered before the soul feels free to lift to the heavens or other worlds.

This delay on Earth may last only a moment or a long time. A soul cannot lift until it feels free of the past.

So the message will be given but only if the soul wants to read the message?

The message will be read by the angels who also know the thoughts of its author. These thoughts will be given to the soul in heaven. If the soul, who also understands these thoughts, wants to read the message, it can do so.

This is a decision of the soul from the point of all understanding. There is hardly ever a time the soul refuses to read the words sent. Some souls may want to move from the earthly ways and put the past behind them. This can be done.

You need to write. The dying of the body is not to be viewed from the perspective of Earth. It is to be viewed from the vision of angels — we see all the heavens and all the worlds — to know the beckoning of the gods who need this particular soul. The ways are clear for the soul to proceed to its next mission.

The life you are leaving is a prelude to the true existence you are entering. You will be received into the heavens. Don't be afraid. This life is only a necessary interim before entrance into a more glorious existence.

All you have loved and adored in this life will again be known. You are now to give this body. You are to free the soul unto God and God's creations. This body is not you. You are the soul.

You are journeying to the heavens and to your blissfulness. Don't be afraid to leave the body. Go forward when called to lift to the Lord. Wonders await you. Much will be understood as the soul rises.

You are rooted in this earthly existence. Set yourself free to know all of God's plans for you. Many worlds and many heavens exist for you.

Treasure the moments on Earth, but know your soul is needed in the heavens. True joy, true happiness, and true contentment await you.

Lifting to God

How can we be with God?

The new way to be with God is to live as if you are in the presence of God. Now each soul will behave in a manner befitting God's creation of the human soul. Be the best version of God's creation you can be. Be as if God is right here with you at this moment.

The way to achieve this will be to know the angels are always with you. Return the love they send you. Be aware of their presence.

We are the holy angels of God. We want only to guide you through life and lift you to God when the time is ready.

Give your thoughts each day to God. This will connect the love from the heavens to you. Send thoughts you would want God to hear. Plan the life you want with the help of the angels around you.

If each person in the world planned his or her moments as if God were watching, peace would come to the world. Make the world your domain rather than fitting into another's mold for you.

Be free in your actions. Be as you desire. Be in the world God created for you. Be an individual. Create your own world. Live as you desire to live. Let no one rule over your actions, as you are in accord with God.

Are guilt feelings retained after death?

Yes, to a degree. The memory of the past life is reviewed and remembered. The feelings are retained in the mind. The angels will help the soul rid its mind of any feelings that are not desired.

Guilt is one of these feelings. The soul may desire to make amends for any pain it caused during its earthly life. At times, this pain is forgiven by the one who suffered it, and both souls laugh about it. The ambiance is lighthearted in the heavens.

Dwelling on happenstance past is not part of the heavenly life. You must forgive yourself for your ignorance in the past. Only when you deliberately hurt another with full knowledge of your actions and their repercussions are you affected.

Ignorance of right action is dismissed and let go from the memory. Guilt is a burden one feels only to hamper growth. Guilt is to be forgiven within the mind.

What is eternity as it relates to us?

Eternity, in relation to humanity, is an unending life growing fuller and deeper with each enriching experience. Death and birth are experiences that enrich the fullness of each of you. You walk through your lives into forever.

All can live more joyously in continued progression. Your present life becomes more and more fulfilled. When looking at experiences from a larger perspective, your lives seem only a moment in time as you rise higher and higher into greater love and understanding.

Is there birth and death in heaven?

No, it is the soul returning to its maker. It is a repose of the soul into blissfulness. One may remain in the heavens or may venture out into other worlds to be born in a physical body.

Heaven is much more than people imagine. There is life, laughter, adventure, and creation, all in an atmosphere of completed joy. A glimpse of heaven is given in your dreams, but you do not remember it.

The life after this life is so wonderful and very much filled with love. A most glorious life awaits you, for you will be welcomed by loving angels. Allow the angels to lift you from this life when the moment comes. Know all the angels of God are here to help you lift to God. This is not a death. This is a new life of all you have ever dreamed. Open your heart to embrace this new life.

Understanding Life on Earth

How do we judge ourselves?

Your angels are with you to make known the reality of the heavens. When the end of life on this Earth is nearing, mortals will want to change their lives and become wonderful. This is good, but the whole life is watched. We don't judge, but you will judge yourself. We will be with you to help with the moments of sorrow.

You will desire to repent when you know the end of your life is coming. The thoughts and feelings of your entire life will be seen again if desired, and your soul will decide where it should reside in the heavens. You place yourself.

When you watch your life on Earth, guardian angels will be with you to help you understand and feel. This will be a most emotional reflection. This will be done in the opening of the heavens.

The past cannot be changed, but from this moment on, your words and actions can be amended to those of kindness. Your life can now be lived as if God were with you. This is your choice. Let this be.

Can a soul be reborn again on Earth immediately after death?

Yes, this can be done, but it is rare. One generally wants to rest and renew to decide whether being reborn is truly what is desired. If there is immediate rebirth, the soul may remember much from its previous life on Earth.

If a soul is reborn on Earth, does it go into the same family line?

Yes, almost always if a soul returns to Earth, it will ask to be born in the same lineage. This is the most comfortable option for the soul. The soul will ever seek happiness and contentment. The familiarity of the traits and culture of what has been known will be more comfortable for the soul reentering Earth.

If the soul lived on Earth before, it may recall fragments of its previous life, either in dreams or in a waking state. Remembrances may filter through the thoughts of the mind. The heritage pulls the soul to it by attraction. Many generations will pass before the soul returns to this family.

If bad feelings exist at the time of death, do they continue?

If errors have been made in life, all reasons for them are comprehended. The life left behind is viewed in a forgiving way. No difficult feelings exist. All is viewed from a more intelligent and compassionate perspective. You are not ever to think that someone who has lifted to the heavens will think lowly of you, because his or her heart is now filled with intense love.

The most wonderful opening and cleansing of the mind will occur in the lifting. Mental problems will dissolve. Understanding will replace any discomfort in the mind. Forgiveness will be given to enemies. Wisdom will replace ignorance. Love will permeate all thought and memories of the past.

Loved Ones

Will a soul be reunited with a loved one in the heavens?

You will not be afraid when it is time to depart, because you know of the wonders of heaven that are waiting for you. There are situations on Earth in which one has loved another so deeply but has not experienced the wonder of this love in return because of circumstances, death, or other factors. When two such souls reunite in heaven, forget any preconceived ideas of what it may be like. There are no words to describe the intensity of the love exchanged. It is more meaningful and more magnificent than anyone could possibly imagine.

When two souls who love reunite in the heavens, wonders occur from the intensity. Could love for another be stronger or more intense? Would you whisper the name of your beloved? Meet this soul in heaven and you will open the sky with your love.

When you call out the name of your love, we search the universe to bring you together. When we look into your heart, we know the love is real.

What can you say to those who mourn the loss of a loved one?

When a soul leaves Earth, we ask you not to try to keep it bound to Earth. Look at the situation in a larger way. Try not to think of your own loss. Think of the soul lifting into blissfulness.

You will be with this soul again in a loving way. Know this: The time will not be long before you are together. Do not mourn the loss of those entering heaven, for they are more blissful than anyone on Earth. They care about what is left behind on Earth. Complete understanding is revealed so that they know they will be with you again. Many watch from beyond to make sure loved ones are comforted.

What of our lives on Earth is to be viewed in heaven?

All thoughts, all words, all actions, and all movement is recorded so that you can view them. The ways are to be given in the opening. What would you want to see in your life? What would you want your guardian angels to view? You may want to live this now and for the remainder of your life.

Clear the mind of hate, contempt, fear, and avarice — all that is not you in your perfection. Be the wonder you are meant to be in your soul. Be the alive soul, the aware soul, the benevolent soul, and the compassionate soul that is the real you. This is the soul you are in the heavens. The eternal soul will be experienced in the heavens.

This soul is not held by the irritants on Earth. Shed the factors that hold you from elevating your soul. Lift to be with God and the angels on Earth. God, the Holy Spirit, and the god Jesus will stand before the souls who pray to give these blessings. We will be with your souls. We stand with the souls who ask God from deep within, the souls who bless God from sincere hearts. The words may not be heard consciously by the ones whose souls say them, but be assured that the prayers are heard and received.

CHAPTER NINE

Heaven

No soul is so lowly as not to be lifted to a place in God's heaven. The soul exists through all lives, all spheres, and all existence. The soul shall never cease to exist in all realms. The mind of the soul integrates with the mind of the body to become the same. The heart of the soul integrates with the mind of the body while the body is living. This is what the whole person experiences.

The not-so-felt soul is encompassed with the human body. The mind tends to feel it is only the body, but it is not reality. The eyes of the body are also the eyes of the soul. The body deteriorates but the soul shall never deteriorate. Age is an experience that the soul must endure.

The people of Earth must touch the soul within to integrate with the body. The eternal soul is one with God. The feelings you have experienced are a way to view the soul. Let graciousness and compassion free you from the shackles of the body's shell to know the true self.

Love is the way to know the true self, which is the soul. The most important way to experience the soul is through the love of God, compassion toward others, and experiencing the feelings flowing from the soul. This is your true self. May each soul on Earth lift to integrate with the body. The most valuable moments on Earth are — now and forever — being the self.

Experience the self to fully integrate the body and the soul. The way to do this is to understand that you will live through eternity. This life is not the only life you will experience. When the body dies, you will be alive. You will be aware of things, of all feelings, of all experiences. You will know your truest desires and purposes. Your awareness will be immense.

You will experience your truest self and will be in a state of joy. Imagine experiencing this while in a human body. This may be done to a degree on Earth. The soul thinks, feels, and knows things. The body is only a shell of the physical, used for the expression of the soul to realize this is a way to be the soul you are and live as this soul.

The Longing for Heaven

Please talk about death in order to alleviate fears.

A lovely garment is given to bestow the glory of the soul as it is ushered to meet God and to the heavenly abode. When he enters, a man may be honored as a great husband or father. A woman may be honored as a wonderful mother or wife. All things will be made right according to the desires of the soul. Earthly wiles do not have meaning unless this is desired.

We are now planning the descent to Earth to alter the ways of humanity. It is a magnificent life in the heavens. It is the same feeling as the aliveness felt in a body. The only meeting of souls is through trust. Feelings are exposed. Nothing is hidden from view. No monetary system is used. It is not needed. Now all things, all desires, are around you and used as needed.

There is a hunger on Earth for something indescribable. This is a longing for heaven. If there are food or wonders not describable on Earth, they are known in the heavens. You know life in the physical body. This movement of the soul called death is only transference from one existence to another.

The real life is not this life. The real life is your next life. There is no fear of letting go in the real life. Humans of Earth lack understanding of what will happen. Some feel all life will cease to exist. This is not true. All life will open before you. When the soul comes close to feeling this, it is so slight that the soul can reach toward God or may return to the physical body. In a split second on Earth, this decision is made. It is a gentle pull toward God taking only a split second. The soul always lifts toward God, toward bliss, toward happiness.

This movement is like a pulling out of the body to lift into blissfulness. Is there a separation? Yes, it is so faint, so subtle, that it is almost indistinguishable. A child may lift more readily than an adult, as the heavens are remembered and there is no desire to stay on Earth, as an adult might experience. Adults often see life on Earth as their reality. They do not want to lose their lives, because it seems like everything to them.

The more the soul is godlike, the more the soul is swiftly lifted to the heavens. The soul will not tarry on Earth. Do not ever fear the death of the body. The body you will have in the heavens is not physical as it is on Earth. It is a perfect soul illumination with the same thoughts, feelings, and desires you experience now. You are all perfection, filled with the light of God. You are the most perfect you that exists. You are any age or no age. You will be seen by others as in a physical body.

The moment of the end of life on Earth is the moment of glimpsing the blissfulness of the heavens. The wonders of the heavens await all who wish to enter. The joys in the heavens are more sacred, more lovely, and more joyful than can even be imagined by any soul on Earth. This is a choice of the soul at the final second of life on Earth. The body shelters the soul from experiencing extreme feelings.

When a soul enters heaven, is it still aware of Earth and earthly things?

Remembrances of the life lived exist but only as glimpses of loved ones at varied times. Souls in heaven can come to Earth to see loved ones or to give messages, but their lives are now in the heavenly realm. They have much to do in the heavens but still adore their loved ones on Earth. They no longer dwell on the Earth plane. They no longer desire to live in the past. These souls live in the heavens but know of their lives on Earth.

They may inquire of souls on Earth or of the angels, but they are not earthbound. Their lives on Earth are over. Love for others will keep them aware of Earth. They want to begin the new life in the heavens without encumbrances. When these souls are received in the heavens, questions regarding things of Earth are answered by the Men of Decision. The Men of Decision will help relate any necessary communications between the lifted soul and any soul on Earth. Letting go of the body to lift to God is something a soul on Earth should try to learn.

As much explanation as needed will be given to souls before they are lifted to God. A soul may need to assimilate what is occurring. It may want to reflect on its past life on Earth or discuss that life with others. When this occurs, the Men of Decision help the soul understand its past actions. They help the soul make further decisions. Time is not a factor in the heavens. The soul may view its past life on Earth and see itself at moments through its life. It will understand why specific things happened. It understands the thoughts and feelings of others as it views life.

The soul sees it as one would see a dream. This is viewed in a dimensional way so that all is understood from varied ways. One may want to see certain parts of life many times. We guide the soul through many phases after the lifting.

The soul knows all they have done in its life to hurt anyone. It knows the truth and will want to make amends to the souls it has hurt. The truth of all things is known clearly. A loved one may know about any soul. Nothing is hidden. Thoughts are not usually known on Earth, so it is difficult for one on Earth to completely understand the workings of how its life will be viewed or known.

Is the transition — the opening to the heavens — a joyous place?

The opening is a difficult place for many souls. They still have all feelings and remembrances from life on Earth but don't understand why they are not yet in heaven. They want to talk about life and why they had to experience the pain they endured. They ask, "Why can't we go live in the heavens?" They watch their past lives unravel before them and need time and patience to assimilate all that is happening to them and around them. One single soul on Earth can hold them to this area because they want nothing in the last life left unfinished. Full understanding of all things must be achieved.

Many need counseling from high souls, angels, or the Men of Decision. They may remain there as long as it takes to assimilate their feelings and understand fully. Some souls transform immediately while others have many questions about life on Earth. The soul is not rushed. The soul may stay and feel all emotions. Only when you feel ready will you meet God and be ushered to the heavens. All help needed is given. Many souls need help with their many concerns.

As Your Soul Is Lifted

Can you tell me about the lifting?

Understanding is given in the lifting. When the last breath is taken, the angels surround the soul to lift to the true life in the heavens. Any fear of leaving the body is dispelled in an instant. Understanding the feelings of others is known. The views of all past experiences are felt in an instant. Fears are replaced by ecstasy unknown on Earth. Angels are with the soul in every way. The most important movement is the love sent to all on Earth at this time.

The mind and soul are completely integrated. Thoughts and feelings are in their purest form. Minds on Earth are in the embryonic stages of perceiving either the voices or images of spirits and entities surrounding them. You are still you. You are your truest self. The development of strong, deliberate thought in the mind is yours. Love is felt more deeply because thought, feeling, and love are all one.

It begins with the reality of death. Why wish to stay in a deceased physical body when the heavens promise bliss unrealized in this earthly plane? You should not take your own life, but a variety of extensions to prolong a life of pain is not warranted. You should realize the physical difference between life and death is a breath.

Existence is and shall ever be in invisibility because of the molecular arrangement. This is the separation between mortals and those who have passed from the physical body. One who has died in the body may be standing beside you this very moment. You are not judged by these souls, only viewed. This may be done in many ways through the mind's vision or dream state.

What are the feelings during the lifting of the soul?

The soul can think, feel, and speak. The individual identity of a person is not lost with the loss of the body. The realization that you are still you in all ways is evident. Life and feelings of love are still yours. You are not a shell of your body. You are you in all ways. You laugh, sing, and dance, but you are more blissful than on Earth and are filled with wisdom and understanding.

You may desire to move through the heavens, and this can be done. The heavens are so delightful in all ways. One may wish to abide there into eternity. One may desire to go to another world and be born into a body. The lifting reveals desires of the soul not before addressed. These are now made clear and may affect future decisions. If the soul lifts to one heaven and is not content, it may move or change as desired. A way to see the heavens will be given to those desiring this. We give images of heaven to some in dreams.

Lifting the soul reveals the knowledge needed to choose the level at which the soul will feel the most comfortable. All knowledge is given in the lifting. The understanding of all emotions, feeling, and words, and deeds is attained. This is a lifting toward God. One may view all levels of heaven. This is a wonderful experience. The lifting will make all quandaries clear in the mind.

This initiation is truly a wonder. The expectation of this experience is enough to lift the soul from the shackles of Earth. This love can be felt for another soul on Earth. If this can be experienced, let it begin. Feel the love if it can be felt.

Love is the most important feeling a human can experience. The love felt is also known by the angels around that person. The most valuable feeling experienced by the soul is the opening of the heart and its integration with the mind. This propels the soul to God. This can be felt by the souls of Earth, even in its low atmosphere. A love felt on Earth will be magnified many times in the heavens. It is a wonder to experience intense love on Earth.

When the last breath is taken, the angels surround the soul to lift it to true life in the heavens. This is a sweet emersion into blissfulness. The scents of the worlds beyond are wafting. The glories of the worlds are visible. Love, deeper than can be found on Earth, is felt in the lifting. Life on Earth becomes a dream state and life in heaven is the true existence.

Any fear of leaving this body is dispelled in an instant. The understanding of the feelings of others is known. The views of all past experiences are felt in an instant. Fears are replaced by ecstasy unknown on Earth. The joys experienced are beyond any feeling ever known on Earth. Angels are with the soul. Life is experienced in clear and full respect. The soul is in complete love and ecstasy.

After this, what happens to the soul?

The soul is brought to heaven. When it is given words, it will ascend to a place where it is comfortable and can enjoy happiness. Souls in a sorrowful state can be helped to know of God's love. When they experience this, they will want to change their behavior.

Souls who do not want to enter heaven will not be forced to do so. We ask all souls. Heaven lifts you to wander the worlds, finding every possible joy. While a soul explores, we watch with wonder. We wait for the soul to lift to the lofty place of its making. This place is our gift to the soul. It is more wonderful than the mind can create. It is a gift of God. When this place is entered, a soul plays as a child or plays as a joyful adult, whatever is desired.

Being in Heaven

Where is heaven?

Heaven is not one area. It is many ways on many levels. We will tell you it is far from Earth. It is not just above Earth. It is physical at many places. It is not like Earth. Earth is the lowest of all living worlds in the universe. It is not lower than the ways of the dark forces, but it is a lowly world.

The physical locations can't be described, as people of Earth cannot map the areas. Let it be known that the heavens are not to be visited by travelers from other worlds. Many realms are so fine in density, they cannot be seen from any location.

Is heaven a place of transition?

Heaven might be a place of rest before going to another life and always a home to return to. A soul may remain there forever or go to new lives. We don't think of heaven as transitory. It is wonderful and eternal. Heaven is wonders without end. When souls leave behind their families, the families may join them in heaven. It may be a place of eternal joy. It may be a place to plan new lives. It is the choice of the soul.

Is there day and night or light and dark in heaven?

Yes, if it is desired. Light radiates from the gods and other beings in the heavens. One can experience multicolored light or darkness if such contrast is desired. This is all part of the realms of the heavens, as is warmth and coolness.

The mind in heaven can create circumstances and surroundings. This is endless, so any feelings or desires can be accommodated. One may desire to experience thunder and lightning or the sound of ocean air and water. All is experienced through thought and desire. Darkness may be a cool repose one may at some time desire. It is then done as desired.

Is there entertainment in heaven?

Yes, if that is what is needed. The thoughts of the mind are very different from those on Earth. A main movement in the heavens is to weld with God. The activities of each soul develop it in areas of interest in preparation for future lives.

All are active in the heavens. The souls learn and develop new skills. Much activity and much knowledge occurs in the heavens. Much of what is gained is retained into the next birth. Some remain in the heavenly plane while others prepare for lives in other worlds.

Do we sleep in heaven?

No, sleep is not necessary, as it is a recuperation of the physical body on Earth. Rest can be experienced if desired. You will not need the physical and mental rejuvenation of sleep in the heavens.

Does heaven have weather?

The heavens are all perfection. Storms are not needed in heaven. There are rivers, streams, and waterfalls, but they are rivers of light and color. They are rivers of pure energy. We see waters when we look into the rivers, but it is all light and color. The colors are brilliant and varied, sparkling and moving.

We have swirls of energy to create that appear somewhat like wind — but no wind you experience on Earth. Rain is a much-utilized occurrence. We use this in many worlds besides Earth. A type of rain is experienced in heaven, but it is energy. It is so beautiful. It sounds like the rain of Earth. We love to make rain because it is so blissful.

Thunder and lightning only happen on Earth, and you remember the occurrence from the creatve powers in the heavens — not the creation itself, but the energies in the heavens. They are almost the same as the thunderstorms on Earth. A soul on Earth remembers these occurrences and is moved by the similar effect.

Are there oceans in heaven?

Yes, you will experience the sensation of salty ocean waters if desired. The heavens are made to enjoy any desire of nature. These are sensations one likes to feel and see. All is given.

The world of Earth has sunshine, trees, and mountains, and all these things we love are experienced in the heavens. All comforts of Earth will be given to all who reside in the heavens.

Do we retain our memories in heaven?

Yes, this can be done if desired. Some souls want to forget life on Earth and begin anew. Others are hampered by visions of life finished on your planet. This can be made clear in a way we describe as welding freedom. The soul can do either.

The soul does not want to be hampered by memories in the heavens, but some souls plan new lives on Earth or on another world. We do not interfere with the soul's desires. If the soul desires, memories can occur to reflect on past actions in order to plan future lives.

Levels of Heaven

Please describe the highest levels of heaven?

In the highest level of heaven, there is beauty unimaginable. Love lifts the soul to this level. There are glittering waters. The overwhelming love and ecstasy is felt all around. This is where the angels meet to plan celestial love and sing celestial songs. Souls visit the wonders of the heavenly worlds. You see mountains, valleys, and streams — all with beauty unfathomable.

God is with those who have this wonderment about them in this most sacred of places. You are with God in a vessel of wonders unimaginable. You build worlds and universes. With the powers of creation, you become as a god in the highest realm of heaven.

Words cannot explain this. It is beyond explanation. It is beyond words. In heaven, there are gardens of perfection with flowers indescribable. There are palaces of gold and beauty of the highest in this level of heaven. All things are perfect, and bliss is everywhere. You are immersed in love! Can you imagine the ecstasy of this?

Can we live in the highest heaven?

God is watching the growth of each soul on Earth. Earth gives you the choice to grow in character to lift toward God. Use this time wisely. When the time comes to lift to the heavens, you will see a high heaven and say, "I want to live there," but you have not become as the souls in that heaven. When your life on Earth was lived, perhaps you did not try to be better and wasted your days and nights in useless banter.

Perhaps you delved into pleasures of the lowest. Perhaps you cursed God and tried to be a person of bitterness and pain. You would not be comfortable in the higher heavens. Pray. Pray now for God to help you be a better soul. Make a promise to God. Keep the promise. Be kinder, nobler, and stronger; be the way you envision yourself in the highest. This can be done. Let not one more moment go on in lower thoughts.

Lift to God. God and the angels are watching you, and they will rejoice at your resolution. Be all you are capable of becoming on Earth. When this is done, you will be elevated. Your soul will be elevated. The most wonderful life lies ahead for you in the heavens. Joy beyond expression awaits you as you are lifted toward God.

The heavens in all strata are so lovely. You will desire to live there for eternity. Even the lowest of the heavens is more beautiful than can be imagined. As the heavens become finer and finer, they are filled with higher entities. When you lift to the heavens, you know where you feel most comfortable.

The heavens are sweeter and more blissful as you are lifted higher. When celestial heaven is attained, one is close to God. The gods may live in this kingdom. It is a heaven of all who are completed in the soul's love. Blissfulness beyond comprehension exists in these heavens. This has been experienced on Earth momentarily by some souls, but it cannot be sustained.

What is the name of the highest heaven?
It is called Yeletet. This is the name as it translates on Earth. This is a heaven of the absolute highest. God and all the gods under the one God reside in this heaven. No other beings reside there except the gods of the heavens. This is a heaven of only gods appointed by the heavenly father. This is true.

There aren't any emotions, any words, or any feelings to describe this heaven. This is above all. This is the ultimate heaven of all heavens in all ways. This heaven is so intensely beautiful, it defies description. We have been taken there to view this and feel this. We were honored in our realm to receive this invitation. This was more than a soul of the highest or of any dimension ever knew.

This heaven was in the ecstasy of emotion, the light of God, the finest, sweetest, most tender love and sound a soul could ever imagine. This heaven is all in every way. The glimpse of this will stay with us throughout eternity. If a soul knew this, it would cry blessings to God every second of its life.

On Earth as in Heaven

Are our actions on Earth meaningless in heaven?

Not at all. All actions performed on Earth and all thoughts on Earth are known in the heavens. The past is done. It will not recur. Movements, feelings, thoughts, and motives of action are all brought forth in the opening of heaven. These affect the level of heaven in which a soul will reside, thus the level of joy a soul will feel. A soul in the opening may feel guilt for past actions. These actions will be understood in all ways. When the soul is administered to in the heavens, it is still aware of past actions and can see and hear all on Earth if desired.

The soul will try to lift to higher levels but the heaviness of the soul from past actions will keep it bound to a specific level or area. The admissions of actions, the invitation of forgiveness, and the opening of the heart all lighten the soul to lift higher. All actions on Earth affect the ways in heaven. The ways, the memories, the feelings — all are considerations of the mind. Attempts to do good works on Earth are watched by the angels. The gods also see these works.

Do souls in heaven know when they have falsely accused someone on Earth (in their past lives)?

Yes, they know the truth and will want to make amends to the souls they have hurt. The truth of all things is known clearly. A loved one may know all about any soul. Nothing is hidden. Thoughts are not usually known on Earth, so it is difficult for one on Earth to completely understand. The workings of their lives are known, feelings are felt, and actions are understood. They can go forward or backward in their lives on Earth. They can understand any person's thoughts and feelings. They know many ways to look at lives.

They cannot change what has happened. The past has been accomplished. This is not changeable. This is finished. They can try to help you if they choose. Many ask angels around them to help them convey their love to people still living on Earth.

We want to tell you a story about a woman who wanted to go to the highest heaven, but the angels wouldn't take her there. She complained and complained to no avail. She wouldn't leave Earth because she wanted to reside there, so we told her that the angels would go to the highest heaven and ask if they would let her in. We asked, but they said no; they would not let her in.

She rested on Earth for hundreds of years and would not leave. We asked her to come with us many times before we went to God. God said he wanted to see her. She went to see God with a needful and humble manner. He waved the requirements and let her into the highest heaven. Finally, she was there. Soon it became apparent that she was not comfortable. All the souls were higher than she was. She was not happy there, so she asked to go to a lower heaven.

Yes, this really happened.

Animals

Do animals go to heaven?

Animals go to a world of their own called Walken. This is a resting place for the animals. They usually want to return to Earth or go to other worlds. We watch over the animals. When they are ready to go to a new body, they often return to Earth.

Cats, dogs, horses, and gentle animals may enter heaven at their will. Only the more ferocious animals live on the world of Walken. When they desire to be made into gentler animals, the angels can help them. Some stay there, some go to different worlds or return to Earth. There is no human life on Walken, only ferocious animals.

This is a world without end. Animals will always be there. Man-eating animals eat the Walken energy, which appears as meat. When they come back to Earth in different bodies, they grow spiritually and intellectually in many ways until they reach the status of a human. We may let some of the animals come to visit the souls in heaven. We watch over them as we do people and let them play. Walken is a world where groups of souls of varied animals live until they return to Earth. Wild animals will change into a higher species each time they return to Earth.

Domestic animals will be in the world above so that when they die, they may roam heaven. Animals are most needful souls and will go through many bodies before becoming human. Love is brought to Earth in many ways. Animals as pets open the hearts of humans to know beings dependent on them for food and affection. This is a necessary growth for some people.

We need ferocious beasts to teach things to people that they need to know. A purpose might be to make one aware of his or her surroundings, prepare for future changes, and quicken the senses for events in future lives. All things on Earth have purpose.

Soul Abilities

Can souls come to Earth to visit as people who have lived in other times in the world?

Yes, this has been done in many instances. These souls travel to Earth to evaluate varied factors. The transmuted souls may have lived in another time and have come to Earth to observe particular events or worldly mentions. Many will do this during all times on Earth. They behave as humans, with needs and wants, but do not live out their lives on Earth.

Can any soul move between states of being solid and transparent?

This is a question about the movement of the appearance from invisible to slightly visible to completely visible. This transformation of the figure is achievable after the death of the physical body. The more evolved the soul, the easier the possibility of appearing. The angels or higher entities in the heavens easily move from one form to another. It is difficult for others, as it is a learned process.

Souls may appear in the dream state, during a vision, in reality, or in vivid, colored light. The transformation of the entity is done by force of thought. The way this is done by angels is through thought, but with lower entities, it is a learned procedure and takes much effort.

Those who have not lifted to heaven but have no body cannot appear except as specters. Those who reside in the heavens or on other worlds can learn this technique and can appear either as specters or as physical beings if they have learned how to do so. The way this is done is through teachings from the angels. Thought can manipulate the movements of particles to let one appear.

Just because the figure appears does not mean the souls of Earth can perceive the entity. Should something be shown with them, as an object, it is only of the heavens and cannot become reality on Earth.

If the soul in heaven can create anything, can it create its own physical body?

Yes, but why would the soul want that? The heavens become less dense and are finer and finer as you become closer to God. The physical body is a heaviness one would not wish to lug around in the heavens. The subtleness and fineness is sought as it lifts you higher toward God.

Do souls fly in heaven?

One can project the soul anywhere. It does not fly in the manner you understand but rather propels itself by thought to any desired place or to be with any desired soul. There is no gravity as on Earth, so you may float about or walk as desired.

Movement in the heavens is whatever the soul desires. Organization is prevalent throughout the heavens but rules do not exist as on Earth. The soul gravitates to what is most comfortable in order to give it the most joy and comfort. The soul finds where it is most comfortable.

Can souls in heaven help those on Earth?

Emotions can be high when entering the heavens. When one has an audience with angels, requests are often made, particularly regarding the past life. Many souls beg to give wonders to their loved ones on Earth. These souls are not embodied by the heaviness of the physical or by the pull of the heavy Earth. Their begging is not for their own souls but for others affected by their lives on Earth.

They plead from the heart of the soul. This is one wonder for which a soul cannot prepare. The soul feels the nucleus of God within itself, and it realizes the true self. When this realization arises and the thought is still for another rather than yourself, this is love beyond imagining. You know the true strength of the soul.

Do the souls in heaven know the thoughts and feelings of those on Earth?

Yes, they can go forward or backward. They can know the feelings of a person in a conversation that took place many years before in life on Earth. They have clear a understanding of all things. They know what will take place in your future. They can read your thoughts at this moment. They fully understand the thoughts and feelings of any soul on Earth. They know many ways to look at lives. They can visit Earth or can watch from the heavens, viewing the past, this moment, or the future.

They cannot change what has already happened. The past has been accomplished. This is not changeable. This is finished. They cannot change the future, but may help you if they choose. Many souls in heaven ask their loved one's surrounding angels to help or to convey their love to a person still living on Earth. Many ways of communication may be embraced.

Materialization on Earth and in Heaven

Are people on Earth given physical gifts from heaven?

No, there are no gifts manifested in heaven that are brought to Earth. This is not done. The wonders that occur on Earth are from angels surrounding that person, not gifts from a heavenly plane. The desire to communicate with those who have left Earth is great. This is not the time to encourage such communication because it will keep the thoughts of the soul here for a time.

A soul needs to go to the heavenly abode to begin the work of God. The people of Earth must let the soul be received in the heavens. It is difficult to let go of the soul, who is loved greatly on Earth. This is to be done. A soul who leaves Earth still remembers life on Earth. Communication should not be encouraged. The soul must be free of encumbrances. Know that all loved ones are reunited in the heavens. If they come to you, receive them and be aware they love you.

Calling to the souls who have lifted will bring them to you, but they have a real life in the heavens and must be free to live that life. They do not bring physical gifts to you. They do not manifest money or things of Earth. They are with the heavenly entities and need nothing of Earth.

They care about their loved ones on Earth and will watch their lives, but they will not bring them things of the heavens. When a soul is lifted, the souls remaining on Earth will want to speak to the lifted soul. This is shown in dreams or visions to the souls of Earth. A way to be with a loved one is to send love to his or her soul. This will be felt in the heavens. A soul greatly loved will feel this and be lifted. One day you will know of this. God is with each soul who has lifted to the heavens. We angels know the pain of loss souls on Earth feel.

Can objects on Earth be moved or changed by those deceased souls who want to communicate with the living?

In the world, a spirit can move earthly objects or make them appear. It is a configuration of an object we call a walment. A walment is a way of changing molecular configuration. This can be given to the people of Earth because it is always on Earth.

A way to do this is to see an object as a molecular configuration. We teach those who have lifted to the heavens to change molecular structure. This is a procedure that may also be learned on Earth. In a world of solid-appearing physical manifestations, it is a way of breaking the molecules apart so that the vision sees the individual molecules. This item can be done by extending the size to view the item at the molecular level. This item may be separated and moved to a different position and then reconstructed.

Copper is a metal easily manipulated, easily enhanced, and easily reconstructed. A one-cent coin is of a metal form that a spirit can easily move. This is sometimes done as a way to communicate with humans of Earth — not by angels, but by deceased souls. These objects do not come from a heavenly plane. Things of the heavens cannot be brought to Earth.

Can deceased souls bring things from Earth into the heavens?

The life force on Earth is low. Energies are not able to manifest as in the heavens or on other worlds. In the heavens, all manifestations are possible. Life is everywhere. Energy is abundant. For example, if a certain locket is beloved by a woman in the heavens, she can take this from Earth, literally, and reassemble it in the heavens. An object loved on Earth may be renewed in the heavens.

This cannot be done the other way around. An object cannot be given to one on Earth from the heavens. You will not receive gifts from a soul in heaven that are physical manifestations. You will not be able to do this. They may send thoughts to you, or they may form gifts from physical elements known on Earth, or they may re-create forms on Earth. Nothing can be sent from the heavens. Gifts of values are bestowed, not material things. Material things cannot manifest on Earth.

In the plan to enjoy all things, if you are so deeply attached to a physical object you enjoyed on Earth, it is possible to take it from Earth and renew it in the heavens. It will no longer be on Earth but will be created for all time in heaven. When this occurs, the object is disassembled into energy and reassembled in heaven. Yes, we can duplicate it, but it is not the exact special object. Many times, it is lifted into heaven.

CHAPTER TEN

Meeting God

When and how do souls meet God?

A soul, when ready and prepared for an audience with God, is lifted by the angels, including the angel who was the guardian of its life on Earth. The soul is now ushered to the feet of God and feels the most incredible emotions one can possibly know. This begins after the soul has been readied to move into the heavens.

God is on his throne atop the great steps. The steps are lined with souls in devotional prayer of thankfulness. God welcomes each soul entering heavens and converses with it. A soul may speak with God. This is a most wonderful honor.

We angels glory in the lifting of a soul to meet God. This is a love experience in the purest, highest form.

Complete Bliss

Can you explain more about preparing to meet God?

We prepare the soul to meet God. The soul can don any arraignment it decides is appropriate with the dignity to be in the presence of the one most holy God. The soul adorns the clothing, and the surrounding angels rejoice in guiding the soul to the living God.

The angel of guidance during a soul's life on Earth will stand with its charge as that soul meets God. We usher the soul to the feet of the Father, the one God above all others. The one who stands at the feet of God and does not tremble is the bravest of souls, for God works with the mind and thunders love with a thought. Words are given to the soul that are sacred only to that soul.

We want to tell of a moment in time that will be noted as a representation of one's life. The angels bring one crucial decision of the soul to reflect its growth during that life. This will not be chosen by the soul but by the watchers of the soul. They will present this moment to the gods to help form the level at which the soul can abide and the ways that it will move.

Directions are discussed with the angels and counselors. The moment chosen will show the soul's growth of character. It is with the most considerable thought that this moment is chosen to be given. The soul will realize what importance this moment this had on its life.

Moments are compiled to form the personality and character. The soul will soar into higher and higher development until the moments become fuller and more profound.

How does it feel to meet God?

God is in the finest, most delicate stratum of existence. When one is lifted to meet God, the blissfulness increases, the spectrum of light softens, and the field of perception becomes softer, lighter, and finer.

More subtle than air, than ether, than the most tender existence known; this is the abode of the one God of all. As a soul is lifted, the coarseness and crudeness of the remembrance of Earth is in its mind to contrast with the surroundings. The actuality of meeting God is beyond comprehension as the soul gasps in anticipation.

The mind asks, "Am I worthy to meet God? Am I presentable enough? Am I deserving of this honor?"

Sounds, soft and refined in the most beautiful music imaginable, surround the soul to give life to the mind. The soul feels humbleness and sincerity of the heart as it stands before God, who is all creation, all life, all intelligence, and all energy. Could anything be more intense or more wonderful?

The soul is brought to tears of joy. The comprehension of this actuality is wanting of nothing.

CHAPTER ELEVEN

The Joy That Awaits You

Please share more about heaven.

When one enters the heavens, the eyes open to see all the light and colors. The senses open to feel: to breathe in the fragrances, to hear the pleasurable sounds, and to touch the magnificent reality. In the heavens, the energies about are all creation, all harmony — all love. The soul is amazed at the love that surrounds it. This is deeper and more intense than experienced on Earth. The soul is in a state of euphoria. This is not a temporal state. This stays with the soul.

The true life is life after the lifting of the soul. This life on Earth will be a remembrance as in a dream. The heavens will welcome your home. Your loved ones will await your arrival with wonders waiting. The truth of all things are revealed. All will be well and right in the heavens. This is what awaits each soul lifting from the body.

When this occurs, the heart is full of love. The mind understands all things. The soul is free. The heart and mind are united to know what is right; contentment as not before experienced will unfold. We take you to a place of high esteem, with the most beautiful gardens and the most beautiful palaces. We lift you to a place to view all the splendors of the heavens. You may only enter the heaven you warrant. Any place entered will be full of joyousness; you each will be with beings of your own level.

When the place of your mention is settled and made your own, you may wish to play or help create in the ways you will be taught. Each soul is free to do as it wishes. Make yourself ready to meet God, for he meets the highest and lowest of souls. When the soul has played with all the joys of heaven, it may travel to other worlds, return to Earth, or remain in the heavens.

Ask and You Shall Receive

How does creating work in the heavens?

Those in heaven can choose anything. They can conceive anything new, or they can choose things remembered from Earth. It is possible to create all things in the heavens. Accumulations of things are not necessary nor are they desired. We can show you this one day. You will be given what is asked.

All things of the mind, which is one with God, can be designed to the level allowed. We need or want by thought. You only need to think about something you want, and it appears. You do not want for things in heaven.

People who wonder what lies ahead will be told they will love there as on Earth, but it will be felt much more deeply. The true love of all time will be yours in heaven. You will find your true loves again in heaven.

How is thought used in heaven?

The most important thing about heaven is the wonderful lives to be lived there. God's heavens are the reality, not the end. The heavens begin new lives in complete reality.

This life is a dream compared to the real life in the heavens. The most perfect life awaits you and all who lift to the heavens. Happiness beyond words awaits you. The glories of the heavens are indescribable. A physical body can be desired, and the soul may become as a physical body by thought.

The body is a replica of the soul. It may appear as any age. It may become as you desire. A physical body is not necessary but many may feel more comfortable in a body. This is a place of choices. A soul may attain all desires. When a soul is lifted to the heavens and meets the angels, the feelings are so intense that it's like being in love for the first time. Thought is used to create all things. Thought is directed and so manifests objects. When an object in the memory is desired, it can be created by thought. The heavens are so magnificent that the objects of the past do not matter.

Those in heaven can visit Earth anytime. Some have many powers to communicate but only watch. Many have loved ones on Earth whom they oversee to make sure they are well. The most highly evolved society on Earth was that of the ancient Egyptians. This was a time of intense spiritual growth and communication with the heavens.

The ancient Egyptians took names from the heavens. The spiritual level of communication was defined and clear. They received eternal names from the heavens and used these to name children. There is great organization in the heavens; each soul has a place. Each soul is lifted to its station. Each soul is honored according to its growth, according to God. When a soul lifts to his heavenly state, the angels are in glory. No soul is so lowly as to not be lifted to a place in God's heaven.

The soul finds a comfortable home. It has evolved to a specific state and will want to reside where the heaven supports this level of growth. This is not questioned because the soul knows what brings the most happiness.

Making Love in Heaven

If you have loved two or more people, will you be with just one in the heavens?

When the soul lifts into the heavens and finds its abode, feelings are made clear with no distortion. Feelings for another soul are complete and pure. All feelings become strong and filled with love and bliss. There is no jealousy, no anger, and no sadness. The fullness of heaven fills the soul. Love for another soul is measured, and if it is needed to fulfill the love of the soul, the love is expressed to another. There will be no duality, no secrets, and no falsehoods. Love between souls is a loving tribute to God. Choosing one love over another will not be a factor. The emotions will be completely clear, and all will be right and good.

Lovemaking in heaven is the intense love reflected in touching each other. Souls are meant to love one another. If two souls love each other intensely, they will touch. It is a pure and wondrous act. Many souls love in the moment of seeing each other again because the joy is so intense. This is the merging of their love for each other, not physical lust as on Earth. Since we are light and soul, we are magnetized to like energy.

Do you mean they merge sexually?

Not as on Earth, but the feelings of sexual joining are in the souls and are fulfilled through the merging of souls. Physically, the organs are the same in the heavens as on Earth. The physical body image is the same but the soul resides in the heavens. The physical image is exactly like the human body on Earth, but the love exchanged is mental, emotional, spiritual, and physical in expression.

When male and female souls merge in all ways in the heavens, it is an integration of what one soul feels into what the other soul feels. This is a merging not duplicated on Earth. Nothing close to this can be obtained on Earth. The ecstasy between two souls can be experienced in the heavens beyond anything imagined. These feelings are an expression of the deepest, purest, and tenderest love that can be experienced in the physical merging of the souls. Those who love more deeply than one can imagine may engage, propelled by the intensity of the love. All is known and correct in all ways in the heavens.

The sexual feelings exchanged are insignificant in comparison to the communion of the love exchanged. The love given is of the highest, not an earthly lust as known on Earth. This is the complete emersion of two souls entwined in blissfulness.

These souls are committed to each other by marriage or by a deep devotion. This is not a crude or abhorrent act. These souls are bound together in a movement of committed and completed love. This is difficult for those of Earth to understand. This is an expression of love in its purest, most joyful form.

If two souls love in the heavens and decide to be born on Earth again, do they take the chance that they may not be together because they won't remember?

Yes, they may request to come to Earth to test their love without memory from the heavens. This may be a way to determine the strength of their love. They may not come together on Earth, or they could discover the depth of their love. This is growth of the soul.

The souls will gravitate toward each other during life. Love binds souls together. A soul may not create the desired circumstances on Earth to achieve its desires, but all feelings — all desires — will be known again after life.

Please explain how souls are married forever in heaven?

Many souls who have loved each other through many lives will be joined together in marriage through eternity. This is done if deep love is measured from the souls. The wedding is blessed with all the joys in the heavens. The two souls can reside in the celestial heavens if desired.

God loves and blesses these marriages. The souls you speak of are one with each other and are sanctified by God in the heavens. The marriages can be ordained. Love so deeply felt knows no limits of time. The marriages are sanctified in heaven or in other worlds for all eternity.

Are souls in monogamous relationships in heaven?

Yes, oh yes. Duality of affections decimates the true and completed union between a man and a woman on Earth or in the heavens. Yes, eternal marriages are monogamous. This is true. Eternal marriages exist in the heavens and on other worlds. These marriages are authorized and blessed by God the Father.

Let it be known, eternal marriages reside in the highest realms of the heavens. These marriages are complete and blissful. When this occurs, the mutual love exceeds anything felt on Earth. All in the heavens celebrate the union. The marriages of eternity are of love beyond mortal understanding.

Loved Ones in Heaven

Are our children on Earth also our children in heaven?

They are individual beings, just as you are individual from your parents. You can welcome them with love as they enter heaven. You will remember the lives on Earth with them. The souls who have chosen to be your children on Earth do so through love. Love will be felt, and if the child wishes to remain with the parent, it will be so. Love is what binds souls together. All will be made right.

When one rises to the heavens, angels will greet you. Loved ones will greet you. The joy felt is immense. When all is viewed and understood, the soul lifted will feel a part of the heavens. A soul will know of God's plan for all and will desire to help. There will be no aching for life on Earth. It will be viewed in entirety, but the soul will be comfortable in God's heavenly place.

If people are alone on Earth, are they also alone in heaven?

The wonderful life ahead is not only given to those who are revered, but those who are not loved on Earth. It makes no difference. The love one has ached for, if it is for another soul or if it is the surrounding love, is given to all.

Love is not the most coveted desire. We will explain. Love can be in the form of a great feeling for another soul. This is desired in the heavens as it is on Earth. The soul is pillowed in joyous love and this bliss surrounds it. This makes a wonderful environment for full creativity. One knows the foundation of security and constancy in this love. This can be as fulfilling as a soul love.

Life in the heavens is complete expression in whatever area of desire fulfills you. Don't ever feel you will be lost and alone in the heavens if you felt this way on Earth. Know this is something your soul must experience.

This is not to be deterred. This is to be known now in this life. If there is a pain, experience it, because after this life, it will be no more. Whatever malady you have given yourself in this life, have strength and endurance. You will know what pains you can feel and endure. It would be difficult to understand from a mortal view, but one day, this strength will be known and utilized. Let the world know that all that is experienced on Earth, though not understood at this time, will be used in a later life. All values of the heart will be needed in another place.

This is what will last after the body has withered: strength, love, compassion, kindness, force of thought, empathy, courage, truth, and creation. All these things will live to be a part of your soul. Build these qualities into your life now, and you will be prepared to reach to the highest.

Separation

Why aren't women given the same standing as men on Earth, and will they have the same standing in the heavens?

Women are in the most honored mention in the heavens. They are goddesses and the angels of the most high. In the heavens, they are joyous. The female is a wonderment of tenderness, softness, kindness, and gentleness; loveliness is reached in this most perfect state.

On Earth, patriarchic societies existed from the beginning. Women were used as slaves. They were given no worth beyond childbearing. The worth of women was not employed. In the heavens, no servitude such as this exists. The female is lifted to God and is crowned with all the glories bestowed. The soul has reached the potential of the fullest. The realizations are profound. Those who kept the female in low esteem now see her as an entity in the higher heavens or at the feet of God.

Is gender still a factor when a soul enters heaven?

Yes, oh yes. The soul is male or female in the heavens. Anything different from this is only on Earth or in the hells, if desired. The souls of heaven are either male or female. All keep their individuality, only in all perfection.

Are there different cultures in heaven as there are on Earth?

All heaven is unending. Cultures of souls may cluster together in an area of the heavens if this is desired. Often those who have loved another on Earth will gravitate to the same level in the heavens to be near to their loved one. Whatever gives the soul the most happiness and contentment is given in the heavens, should the soul warrant this.

Considering a coal miner in South Wales, a princess in ancient Egypt, a cowboy in the Old West, are the different eras and cultures of the world duplicated in the heavens?

The loves of life on Earth are replicated in the heavens to the contentment of the soul. This is a love of the soul. Whatever is desired in the heavens is given. The last life on Earth is only one lifetime. Even though the soul resonates with life, many lives have been endured by the soul and many experiences have become part of the soul. When your perspective is enlightened by all knowledge, all remembrance, and all eternal viewpoints, your desires may change. Whatever is desired — even the love of the odors of Earth — are given as desired. Create your desired life in your mind, and it will be given.

Can you tell me to what extent our lives are preplanned, controlled by heavenly factors, or controlled by us?

Life is planned in an overview before entrance by birth. Growth patterns are pointed out and agreed to by the soul. Any afflictions or setbacks are disclosed. The soul may request specific occurrences. All are for specific reasons, often not understood by the soul during life.

When souls are born, they can follow the predetermined path, or they can fight against it. The life path is easier if these are followed. In a world such as Earth, to rebel against the life path is the usual way. This causes turmoil in life.

Heavenly help is given if requested, but we most often do not interfere with the soul's desires. The extent of our involvement is determined by each soul. Each is different. You may spend all your time in prayer. Someone else may fight his or her circumstances with all thought and action. Another may follow the lines of his or her ancestors. The soul alone decides its destiny.

Since life is preplanned, what if a soul goes in a different direction from destiny?

When a soul deviates from destiny, it is of not much consequence. It may live again in the true life of the heavens. Many do not live the preplanned life, as they do not connect with the soul within. Activities of daily life keep the person from feeling what was known in the heavens. Life goes on through eternity, so this short life is not to be taken in extreme seriousness.

Let what has gone before remain in memory only. This is the moment your life can be changed to live what you planned and agreed on with the angels.

CHAPTER TWELVE

Dreams

Author's note: I'm sure that many of you have what are called "prophetic dreams." You dream of something and a short time later, you find yourself experiencing the exact circumstances of your dream. This has happened to me numerous times. Often you can meet loved ones in your dreams.

There are even what are known as "simultaneous dreams." This is when you and someone close to you have the same dream at the same time. There are times you can have dreams within dreams, within dreams, within dreams. (I could go on and on). Dreams give insight to the feelings of other souls. If you have a question about someone or something, you can request this insight to be revealed in a dream. "Does he really love me?" This is a great way to find out.

Yes, I know sometimes we're exhausted and don't remember our dreams. This is fine. Keep requesting, and the answer will come. It's not necessary to ask strangers questions about your life. All you need to know is inside you! Your soul knows everything, travels everywhere (during deep sleep), and can interpret the feelings of anyone.

At times, you may dream you are in a class, being taught by angels. They do take us to places where we are taught the ways of the heavens or some life lesson we may need to learn. Often these are not remembered. Everything the angels do, whether in dreams or in life, is to help bring your soul to God.

Is a soul's quality tested in dreams by angels?

Yes, the soul is watched during dreams to evaluate what the soul will do in varied circumstances, to measure its growth. The way this is done is the angels give desires to the soul to see what is accepted and how it is taken. One can perceive the true actions of the soul. The dreams are a true mirror of the growth of the soul. The reason this is done is to open the heart of the soul to know its own growth. The ways of your soul are known by your surrounding angels. It can be seen if you are a thief, liar, cheater, or deceiver. The true actions of your soul can be perceived. Your dreams are a true mirror of your level of growth. The angels guide you to the tests of the soul by your own request. Your soul's dreams are always watched by entities of the heavens. You may view this after life to help determine the heaven in which your soul would be most content.

The angels might give proof to God of your growth during life. This may be a dream testing. Life can be acted or supposed. Dreams are not feigned or pretended. The actions during dreams reflect the true soul. When a soul dreams, the angels are reading the mind of the person dreaming. Many factors affect the dream. They may be physical, environmental, or mental interruptions, but in the deepest dream state, the soul is free to be lifted by the angels to train in the heavens. If this is to be decreed and the soul desires it, the soul may be lifted to the place where learning is needed.

Angels will always be with you. You are always safe in the soul. Many teachings are given to the soul during the deep dream period. The soul is free to visit others. You may desire to visit a certain place. This can be achieved in deep sleep. Any deep yearning of the soul can be achieved in this state. The body is at complete rest while the soul is active. Teachings are revealed and may or may not be remembered in the waking state.

Remembering Your Dreams

One way to see your dream is to tell yourself you will remember the dream. As you practice, this will occur. A way of seeing is to watch yourself from another point, as if you were watching a movie. Many times, you will call the angels to lift you from the dream to return to your body. Feelings may be intense during the dream. You may test yourself to reveal what you would do in a specific circumstance. You will see your true moral code. Watch others and see how they react to you in your dreams. You can perceive another's true feelings. The way to do this is to reflect on the dream while you are awake. Much can be revealed.

Dreams are remembrances of visits to heaven and other places the soul travels while the body is in deep sleep. Dreams are thoughts of what is remembered when the mind thinks. Pictures and memories flood the senses. One may recall them vividly. Another may only recall bits of memory. Both are valid remembrances. A man and woman who are not able to be together in life can meet in dream images. When they meet, it is as if there are no boundaries and no time limits. The way to experience this is desire.

We, the angels, know all thoughts and all dreams. The images you dream are from your spirit connection with the physical body. Once connected, it is a mirror of your consciousness. A dream is a connection with the world of spirits with no barriers. Your soul may lift out of your body during a dream to await the next phase of your teaching. Angels guide the soul to places of teaching. We will watch and protect the soul during these teachings.

How You Dream

The way you dream is by letting your mind fill with pictures. The way you interpret the pictures is through your subconscious mind. A method of determining the meaning is to not try to evaluate but rather to just be aware of the feelings during the dream. Let the dream happen as it will. The dreamer has control over the dream, but controlling the dream is not advisable. Watch as a spectator and let the dream unfold.

The soul may be with other souls in the dream experience. This is the intent of the soul to satisfy a longing. This may be something unfulfilled in the reality of the daily life. Souls may communicate with help from the angels during the dream state. If the desire to be with another is deep, it may be fulfilled in dreams.

You may visit other places and other times. You may move forward or backward as you deem. You may be shown a period of time in the future that is important for you to know. Memory may pull you to a time in the past. This is not soul travel, but the memory of the mind. Soul travel is possible. The time is not right to unveil this technique. At a time in Earth's future, it will be disclosed to a man named Arewan.

The spirit can travel anywhere when the body is asleep. The main thing is that we must guide the spirit where it wants to go. The spirit is moving in an almost spontaneous lifting and is taken to the place of desire. A spirit may desire teachings from the angels. We help in whatever way is asked of the soul.

Soul travel is as easy as falling asleep. A way to know this travel is to remember when you awake. When you sleep, the soul may lift from the body. We take you to live your desire. If you seek knowledge, we teach you. If you seek love, we bring you love. A soul may be watched for progression and tested for ways to see questions arising. Let them be answered. One thing must be told. A way to see the world is to lift to God. Many things are revealed to those who ask.

Dream Messages

How do we understand the messages of our dreams?

The methods of understanding dreams now on Earth are not really correct. The way to understand your dreams is to feel the emotions of the dream, feel the wants of the dream. These are meant to help the dreamer feel that emotion.

When deep love is felt, a dreamer feels this in the soul. A dream is a way of relieving the mind from stress. The dreams that give us insight are most fortunate, as most dreams are not clear. The feelings and the colors of the dreams are important when trying to understand them.

How can we see the future?

We start by telling you the future can be changed by thought and action if it is not interfered with. If it is not interfered with, the future will be as perceived. You will, rest assured, be made into a seer for your own soul, not for others. Ask to see your future. When this is done, sleep, and when you awaken, write down your dreams. Don't try to interpret your dreams at this time. Do this several times during your sleep periods. You will notice some of the dreams are clear while others are muted.

The clear dreams will foretell occurrences that could happen to you in the future. Later, you will be involved in an action and will remember the action was part of your dream. As this happens more and more, you will find your dreams can foretell what may occur in reality. All of the future can be understood in this way.

CHAPTER THIRTEEN

Thought

Thoughts are heard. Anytime you talk to anyone in the universe, it is received by the other's mind. On Earth, the thought is received but might not be accepted by the other's conscious thought. In other places in the universe, thought is received and accepted because minds are receptive to any communication.

Make no mistake, a thought is more powerful than you could know. Thoughts do more harm on Earth than you can imagine. So it follows that thoughts of love generate wonders in the world. Our wonders are but concentrated love sent to the human mind. We give ideas about wonders. Let all innermost thought be put on paper. As the words are written, the angels watch. Give your deepest love. Send focused thought. Now it will be received. The world will benefit, even if these words are shown to no one. Love is waiting for your wonderful thoughts.

The wonder is this: Your feelings are expressed. Thoughts are released into the atmosphere, and the angels can help you because all is clearly understood. Picture people prosperous and with great joy. Feel their pain and replace it with joy in your thoughts. The recipients will receive this in their minds and souls. This will occur. When this technique can be sustained in your mind, great wonders will begin to occur on Earth.

Creating through Thought

How do we create great thought?

Send one thought of quality, love, honor, or hope. Do not send lowly thoughts. When you have the ability to convey thoughts directly, you will also have the quality of thought to propel. Create your thoughts as if you were creating a beautiful painting. Create joy and lightness in your thoughts. Make only thoughts of greatness or joy.

People's thoughts must lift to another level to prevent pain and suffering of many parts of the world. The world needs the focus of each soul to regain the calmness of the past. We tell you that human society is propagating faster and faster. Souls wonders, "Why are we here on Earth?" The soul and mind as one must develop equally to a higher plane of existence.

Be the one standing tall among the chaos. Keep your life and your thoughts gentle in the eyes of God. This means: Send loving thoughts. When sending thoughts of kindness, the one factor so important to know is that God is here and alive. Now each person on Earth can choose to grow or refrain from growth. This is a choice. No soul is so lowly that God will not welcome the soul as it lifts to heaven.

People's lives belong to you in ways not understood. You must be able to give to others all you are able, to help those who are in need. This lifts your soul closer to God. Lift to God all that is his. You are perfection in the soul. Lift to the great God. Give God all you are and all you will become. God will be so merciful to the children of Earth.

How does thought affect our lives?

Chaos occurs when people's thoughts are inconsistent, weak, and uncommitted. When ignorance and selfish thoughts are manifested, chaos occurs. When intelligent and generous thoughts occur, order and love are the result. You should take great care in the thoughts sent forth from your mind. The whole world will either benefit or war from the thoughts being sent forth. Let the goodness in you dictate your thoughts.

When your mind is saddened or angered, do not let it stay in that thought. Create your life by the thoughts you can create and send out to the world. You can create your own reality. Ask God for wisdom to be the greatest person you can aspire to be. We watch and see what is needed in life. We give whatever is possible. When someone with pain and suffering is gone from Earth, this person's possessions will be given freely. You should help alleviate the pain and suffering not with money but through thought and love. Money will be needed all over the world for many eons of time.

Ask your angels to surround you. Ask God for help to understand your purpose on Earth. Ask for wisdom. Ask for love. Ask to be lifted from ignorance. All these will be given as requested with a sincere heart. Give thankfulness to him. He will respond with angels showering love and tenderness. Those who can lift their hearts and minds to God can bring about wonders in their lives and the lives of others.

If you shelter this adornment from the world, you cannot stand tall in your soul. If you are unadorned by wealth, you can see the human struggle, whereas if you are only immersed in your own belongings, you can see no further than your riches. If you can see the world as it is with eyes of your own glory, you might not view the life of angels for their tenderness and compassion. You are only given eyes of one who has given nothing to the world.

We are not always with the adorned humanity, for its awareness consists only of its surroundings and possessions. We are with those who are aware. We are with them to help in varied ways. Those who seek us will receive attention. People of varied races exist not only on Earth but in many worlds. This is chosen by the soul. A soul may want to endure specific occurrences for its own growth.

Make the most of your life. People of the world will wait no more. You are now finding ways to meet the angels around you. God's plan is to make ready the world for people to live in bliss. All the world will open as a whole if each person sends thoughts of compassion to the others of the world. Care for strangers. Send them love through your thoughts. Direct your thoughts to others with feelings of love.

The suffering of the world will be helped by the mass of love. When walking alone, an individual is with all the thoughts around him or her. Encompassing the person with thoughts of love will shelter this person from all harm. This can be done. Create the world you want using thought and feeling.

Fulfilling Desires

Is it all right to put yourself first?

A self-fixation will bring no blessings or joys except of a temporary nature. On Earth, you always think of yourself first. The achievement of happiness is foremost in your mind. You must step out of this and think of others. The natural movement is to concentrate on the self. If you give thought only to yourself, you will not concern yourself over others. This is not a way to God. If you put the lives and happiness of others over yourself, you will be most blessed.

When the mind realizes your thoughts are only for your own good, you must change the direction of your thoughts to touch the feelings of others. If your thoughts are only directed toward yourself, you keep the mind at a lowly level. To gain wonders in life, your thoughts must progress beyond this.

How do we get what we want?

When a desire is requested, the way must be made clear for the procurement of the desire. Begin by focusing on the calm strength of the soul. Let kindness radiate into care for all in your surroundings. Let respect for God reflect in the organization, the cleanliness, and the harmony of your body, your attire, and your surroundings. Prepare to receive the wonders. Let the extensions reflect the beauty of the soul. When angels enter, give them honor by receiving them in a home of comfort and love. The movement of energy will have a clear way to achieve results.

Wonders normally do not occur in chaos. Prepare yourself and your surroundings to welcome the angels and the miracles. Let prayer to God and thanksgiving radiate to bring these wonders to your home. Expect the glories. Give thanks for them. Be readied in all aspects of life. When all is in order, it makes way for the wonders to occur.

If we leave pictures of our desires out in the open, does this help bring them to us?

You can place a picture and say a sacred prayer for receiving the object. Movements are at work to help receive this. Many are now working to help you. This, as well as writing to the angels, brings these desires to our attention. The mind's thoughts can be scattered and not function in an organized way. We angels can better help when we understand exactly what is desired. Desires change constantly in the mind, so the difficulty of specifically pinpointing the needs and entitlements is unclear.

Material possessions are not to be indulged in constant movement. How does one show a picture of good health? How does one picture growth to God? How does one show wisdom, kindness, or possessions of the mind and heart? Be most careful with what is asked for. These are not to be given to unworthy souls. Make your soul worthy of receiving such gifts from the heavens.

How do we open our hearts to God?

When a movement of love wells inside the heart and when moments occur to move the heart to trembling, the soul readies to aliveness. Feelings are born in the soul. This begins the movement toward God. Feeling is the way to God. This love can be met with thankfulness, compassion, gratitude, tenderness — a movement of love in the heart. To open this great chasm is to unfold the light of God within the soul.

Welcome these feelings, for they bring a tempering of the emotions, a softening of harshness, a gentleness in the movement of the soul. This welds the angels to you in subtle ways. This fuses the music of the heavens into life. God lives in this heart of the soul. The life is within you to experience. This loveliness, this empathy, this discernment, this peacefulness is all within your soul. One needs only to unleash this wonder within. Now one can feel this wonder of God. When this tenderness comes forth, it is reflected in the eyes, the smile, the voice, the movements, the intellect — all. This softening appears in all aspects of life.

How does thought affect the world?

When thoughts are sent forth, they can affect many things of the world. It is the responsibility of each soul to lift the quality of thought. We want humankind to watch words and actions. Be most careful of thought sent into the world. Thoughts are most powerful and can do a lot of harm if not controlled. Leaders would be wise to watch words most carefully. One day, you each will reap the rewards of your thoughts. The wants and desires will be given, so you must be most careful of your desires. Thought is God's gift to humanity to use wisely.

You may direct your thoughts. Choose not to cause pain but to effect joy. Help yourself and others to greater happiness. This influences the future actions of the entire world. When a thought reaches the atmosphere, it can be picked up by any soul with the same mind waves. Thoughts can be sent to any soul, even souls not of this Earth. Direct your thoughts to any soul. Send strong thoughts to this person. They will be received.

If a soul wants to communicate with others, thoughts can be more powerful than words. The thoughts may be waiting for the mind to receive and accept. Thoughts are also transmitted spontaneously and may be received the moment they are sent. When this occurs, the mind responds to thoughts in the atmosphere.

You only need to be aware of interfacing by sending and receiving thought, clear and strong. A soul need not be close to the receiver of the thought to communicate. One way to describe it is to make the thought as strong as possible without saying it aloud. Make the thought defined and clear.

Show Gratitude and Give Thanks

Is the future predestined, or can it be changed by thought?

You need to understand the future of the world. Changes occur with every action. Some things are ordained. When you see the future, you may see these things. Other mentions may differ in duration or circumstance. Many things are changed by thought and by physical action. A tumultuous occurrence may not even come about because of prayers to God. If thoughts are so distraught as to affect the outcome of an occurrence, it indeed may worsen.

Thoughts from the mind cannot be stopped. As soon as thoughts are transmitted from the brain, they may be augmented into positive suppositions. It is not natural to think only positive, good thoughts. When you realize that a thought may do harm, it is easy to defer to another way of thinking. Cause no harm by your thoughts if it is at all possible. Some events cannot be changed but can become less or more by thoughts moving in the atmosphere. Know that thoughts may change time as it is known on Earth and may change events preordained to occur. Thoughts with feeling and emotion may be needed in the world to hamper destined, unfortunate events.

When feeling enters a thought, it becomes powerful. When a focused thought is propelled through the atmosphere, it can initiate changes to happen. A way to do this on an individual basis is to direct your thoughts to a specific person. Picture the person as you wish the person to be, and bless them by sending love. You may do this for yourself as well. A way to attain the one goal you desire is to picture it already attained.

Is it wrong to use thought to receive possessions?

Words are not often said to thank God for all his gifts to people. God gives gifts to all humanity. A child who takes without one passion of thankfulness is no longer given gifts. You should be thankful for what is received. Most gifts come from God and his angels. One day the world will know of God's gifts. A world without help would be a world of desolation. Objects of possession are without meaning. Instead, build your thoughts to alter energy. This will be a power you can have after this life. Make your thoughts strong enough so one with perception can hear your thoughts. Send love and healing to all people of the world who are in need.

It is not wrong to possess many things and build strength within yourself, but to feel the love and compassion for others and send this love to them is much more important. Thoughts can be originated in constructive, powerful, directed ways to change or influence your surroundings. Prayer to God is an example of sending thought. Sincere prayers consist of feeling and emotion with strong, directed thought.

Why do we make so many errors in judgment?

The mortal human is free to err or free to perform correct action. We do not interfere. The mind receives so many thoughts about choosing the easy path for the soul; discretion is necessary. Ignorance is not a trait to be sought, but people often use the way of ignorance because it is a relaxed movement in the mind. If you give thought and consideration to your deepest feelings, you will know the correct action. The easiest path is to examine your thoughts and feelings. This will bring you in accordance with the direct path to God.

The mere thought of gratitude lifts the quality of thought. All you need to do to lift your thought is to feel grateful for anything. Feel truly, deeply grateful. So many wonders come from the heavens. When these come to you, be thankful. Feel this: Do not say empty, hollow words. Feel! Feelings are the true words of God.

When the end of your life abates, forgive the souls who you may encounter. Forgive yourself for your feelings of ignorance, vileness, and hate. Let these die with the withering body. Your whole life is looked at in reflection, so at the moment, let go of all feelings that are not of your perfect self. Dismiss all creations of the mind not of the highest import. Try to forget the maliciousness of others and the jealousies, the fears, and ignorance of the mind. Try to keep the wonder and the love.

CHAPTER FOURTEEN

How to Pray to God

What is the purpose of prayer?

The cause of all despair is in the human mind. We can lift the mind if God lets us. When you ask something of God, your pleas are heard by the angels, all the gods in the heavens, and all beings in all spheres. A plea to God is not a light, insignificant thing. If the prayer is to be granted, the angels convene to discuss it. A realm of angels will decide the outcome. The future of the world can be changed by a single prayer. Many lives are affected by the outcome. All manner of species may be affected. Do not ask frivolously for wants and desires. All actions must have multiple reactions, affecting many lives.

Make the soul understand that prayers are serious. Make the soul know the purpose of prayer. The purpose of prayer is to give thanks to God in the heavens for the goodness he has given you. All comes from God — all. Now the souls on Earth think they deserve of all wonders, but this is not so. All things to support life are from God. All gifts from the one God are to be enjoyed. Give thanks to everyone for the gifts given. When a fellow man gives you a gift, do you not say, "Thank you"? Would you do less for God, who is all? Give praises to God for all things.

Consider the Outcome

When a plea is asked before God, let thought go into the words and feelings before making the request. Ask how the world will be affected by this. The words and thoughts are so extremely important. The prayers and pleas sent to the heavens are most sacred words. Give them with humbleness before God. Give them with feelings and love. Ask in one way for God to issue his mercy on all, but ask in another way that blessings be given.

The most wonderful God will bestow his blessings on you and the world. You may talk to God, but give honor and thanks to him. Those of Earth ask all things constantly without thoughts of repercussion.

It must be known that a prayer is of great importance. Give thanks strongly when asking for a change. Think not of your own needs, but question how this fulfillment will affect others. Know all things will be given to you in the heavens. It is not necessary to have all fulfillment in this life on Earth.

The angels know the sincerity and intensity of the desire. The love given to God will be felt. Let no words without meaning be sent to God. These are solace to the senses, but they are not suitable to send to God. Be of the greatest sincerity when addressing the heavens. Relate the feelings, not only the words. Ask God for gifts to benefit all humanity, not only you.

How can we open our hearts to God?

Directed thought with sincere feeling will open the soul's irregular movement. This vibration or movement in the soul will let tenderness into the heart and mind. The tenderness is a giving of oneself to God. The surrender of the ego will give way to an understanding of the spiritual realm. Giving sincere thankfulness will also open the heart to feeling. The beauty of the soul will permeate the mind and physical body to bring a peacefulness and gentleness to the energy of the person.

Once this has been opened, the way to God is found. There is a deepening of emotion and aliveness in the body and a lifting of the spirit. There is a remembrance of the aliveness of the soul in the heavens. A child has this remembrance, but the soul loses this most precious joyousness over time. To enact this again in a human life is a wonderful feeling.

To touch the core of the soul within and let it rise to the daily activities affects all surroundings. Let the actions of the body not be from a hollow nucleus. Let the actions come from the integration of the soul and the mind. This will bring a softness and aliveness to life. A thankfulness, a wonder, and a most tender heart will be sustained in daily activities. Let the soul open and be vulnerable to the world. The soul is always protected.

Responses to Prayers

How are most prayers answered?

Prayers to God are the most direct communication with God. God will answer in his way, in his time. The moment of prayer is most significant in a communication to the heavens. God sees all ways and knows the sincerity felt. A word of angels is worth the most precious mentions on Earth. When you hear the word of the most sacred angels of God, you are most honored. God hears and understands all ways to talk to him.

All prayers are taken into account and discussed among angels. There are times when angels see a traumatic occurrence as the best way to help. This is rare, but it does happen that a league of angels may intervene in a situation. Events may be altered. Creative change may occur in an instant to permeate wonder on Earth. These manifestations are called miracles. These interventions are not normal occurrences. The movement of all things surrounding must be altered. This will occur if it is decided this is the best way to enact change.

Angels love to work in subtle ways and movements. Much thought is given to each action. Angels enter the sphere of Earth so gently that they are almost undetected until you are capable of feeling the love surrounding you and can understand it comes from the angels.

Can we prayer to our angels?

The prayer is always given only to God. The most sincere and genuine, heartfelt prayer is given much worth. This can be addressed as you desire: "Dear God" or "Heavenly Father," as long as you know the prayer is addressed to God. It can be a prayer of words, thoughts, or feelings. The angels hear the prayers and know your thoughts. They know your sincerity. The prayer may be given to the angels to enact or discuss, but do not pray to us. Pray to God in the heavens.

How are decisions made in answering prayers?

Angels meet to place the directives from God in the proper order of importance. We discuss the most important directives and how to best handle them. The seemingly most insignificant prayer can have the highest power in these decisions. The way decisions are made is that angels will discuss all aspects of the issue. If people of Earth wish to make a plea with angels, they pray to God. This is a most valued decision.

The angels weigh each possibility. The answer may take a long time to be decided. When a decision is made, the angel in charge of the soul will enact the decision. The souls of Earth are not to question the decision of God or his appointed angels.

The court now awaits decisions affecting thousands of lives in the East. If it is the decision to now let the souls lift to heaven, this is how it is to be. We angels are with the souls of the world to help. If it is decreed, a mass of people must lift from Earth. Let it be known that it is for a reason not understood by the souls of Earth. The souls may feel, "Oh, it is a terrible thing for those people to die," but they do not understand the reasons for the directives from God. All these souls may be needed in another place now. The souls are not in sorrow. The souls are in bliss. If it seems this is not the way one should desire, know that the reasons are known by God and his holy angels. They are not a mention of the people of Earth.

Consider that this could change all destinies to lift these souls. All movements of souls — Earth and all things — are because God in the heavens has decreed these movements for purposes not understood by humankind. The single, most important thing they need to know is that the directive from God is all. This is the word. It is to be carried out by the angels.

We are with a most loving God. God is powerful and merciful. God is all. We are honored to be the most sacred angels of God. This is to be with all souls: The word of God is a wonder to be treasured. It is an honor to hear his word.

World Prayer

We are to tell you the words of the great god Abraham. The world is now to meet in group prayer in which each person in the world speaks to God from the heart. This will enact miraculous results. The world needs this prayer summit to help the ignorance and hatred that is escalating globally. Not only should the leaders meet, but you should also arrange the moment when all souls pray in unison to God.

The prayer of the souls should include the elimination of poverty, freedom from ignorance, freedom from fear, wisdom for leaders of countries throughout the world, prosperity and abundance, love, and peacefulness throughout the world. These are not only words. This is to be felt deeply, fully in the soul. This will help in many ways all over the world.

How can prayer help the world?
Though we are always with you, we are not always on Earth. We are now in a place of great thought. This, in terms of Earth, is a sacred place of the magnificent wisdom of God. Here, we meet to take people's prayers into account. We have listened and responded to prayers of the heart. Should a prayer be in accordance with God's will, it will be given as requested.

We would like to explain the most interesting way miracles occur. If the people of Earth pray, each in his or her own way, for a particular occurrence to come about, we meet to discuss how this can be accomplished. Those sending their thoughts into the atmosphere help the accomplishment of their goals, and the angels direct the outcome. Working together, we and the people of Earth can bring about the most wondrous conditions.

If one asks God with a humble, sincere heart, the prayer is taken most seriously in our chambers. Wonders on Earth can occur in this way. As it is, your minds are not focused on positive goals for humankind. Each of you is selfishly thinking how to better yourself or how to receive gifts. Once your minds think beyond their own desires and concentrate on what is needed to help the world, we angels rush in to help achieve this goal.

If it is true that prayer throughout the world can bring about wondrous conditions, can it be obtained practically? Does this contradict the known teachings that Jesus will return to Earth?
This will be obtained in another age when wars have subsided and devastation is all over Earth. People will pray to endure no more wars. At that time, feelings and emotions will be very intense; this will evoke changes in the world through the people's own volition.

This is obtainable now; however, people do not think about other's needs as much as their own right now. It would be most difficult to enact this at this time. People who understand the power and depth of sincere prayer use it not for peace and love in the world but for obtaining their own desires.

How this contradicts the writings about Jesus coming to Earth is that the god Jesus is always and forever watching Earth, as he considers all on Earth as his children. The method of this prayer is revealed to end the warring on Earth and evoke wonders and miraculous occurrences, but the inhabitants of Earth are not going to pray for others over themselves. When devastation sweeps over Earth, then those left will pray for all souls left on Earth. Not until that time will they completely understand the necessity of prayers to God.

Jesus will appear when a time is given. This world prayer can be done now, but it will not be done at this time. It does not interfere with the previous teachings of the appearance of Jesus on Earth. The level of growth on Earth does not uphold the fulfillment of world prayer at this time. The prayer, even if enacted, could not sustain beyond a few moments. The focus of the mind cannot be sustained long enough. The feeling in the soul cannot be sustained long enough. The level of growth in the people of Earth is lowly at this time.

To avert wars, the most sincere and genuine prayer from many parts of the world would have to be given to God continually. People of Earth are too concerned with their own lives to pray for those they do not even know or those who have yet to be born. Let the prayers from your own mind and heart lift your own soul to God. Pray for others through your own soul. This will help. When wars occur across the world, people will fall on their knees and pray aloud for God's mercy. The world needs the highest thoughts and prayers of humanity to lift from ignorance.

Will this deep group prayer ever come about?

There is a woman in the future who will begin a religion of women. This woman will feel so deeply for the men and women all over the world that she will beg others to pray for the maimed and the dying.

The people will gather to follow her and will pray with her. The prayer will bear such astonishing results; others will hear of it and join the prayer. These people will pursue hope for humanity through prayer and the manifestation of deep, strong thought. If people knew the power of clear, strong thoughts and how these techniques can affect the world, they would spend hours developing their thoughts.

Developing Strong Thought

Would you tell me, step by step, how to develop strong thought and obtain desires through thought?

- Write out a desire on paper.
- Read the desire many times.
- Think about the desire.
- Feel this desire has already happened. Feel this! Feel this!
- Simulate how you will feel when the desire comes into fruition, and let this happiness surround you.

This has covenants to abide by:

- No one can be hurt from your receiving this desire.
- The way must be made clear for receiving the desire.
- Only the surface must now be with the mention.

What does that mean?

The living, material result of a desire must be open to the manifestation. This must be clear. The workings of all other plans of manifestation must be in agreement with the result of this request. If one manifestation is not correct, this cannot occur. All must be in harmony. This is something beyond anyone's control. When everything is in harmony to receive the desire, it will happen.

The mind can then achieve what is referred to as a miracle. The thoughts must be of a higher level than is now used on Earth and must be stronger and clearer. As a student of this practice, you must direct your thoughts in a powerful motion, as if you were pulling back to propel an arrow. You aim and shoot at the target. This must be done.

The mind can achieve greatness. Prayer to God is a way of focusing thought. Writing to God or the angels of God is a way of putting thoughts into focus. Of most importance is feeling the movement of the achievement of the desire into reality. Know this will be. Know this will come about! An exertion is necessary for those on Earth to create circumstances to their benefit. Miracles can be attained but only in circumstances where exception is necessary. Lift to God your thought and prayer, but walk on Earth. The physical body is here to use.

Action is necessary. All time can be spent in thought but if thought is not acted on, it is not valid in reality. When the most important goals are your words and thoughts, use physical action to enact the desire. The mention of the physical is not abhorrent to angels. Earth is a physical world. To weep and wail or plead and pray are all ways of achieving things, but they take much time and energy. Asking the divine can bring achievement; however, using your own physical action to achieve a goal is a much-used way on Earth.

Many wonder how to achieve specific goals. The ways are known. Take an action most in alignment with the ways of God. Earth is in alignment with physical action. Bring the physical action to the fore, and use it for the most good.

Human senses and the physical body give the thought and feelings a method of enactment. If you were able to use only thought, you would not be born on the lowly Earth. The body is to be used in the achievement of the mind's desires. Bring the desires to fruition through the combination of thought from the mind, feelings from the heart, and senses and exertion from the physical body. The more the integration is developed, the more benefits will be accrued. Live not only in the mind and heart but in the body's physical action as well. The most welcome influences come from taking action.

Often, thoughts are so vague that they are not acknowledged by unseen forces. An action can be seen and felt. These entities join your energies to help bring about the desire. Action is the gross manifestation of thought. The performance of action in a physical way is a manifestation of thought. In a positive manner, this always brings a flood of repercussions in seen and unseen ways. The physical manifestation is what is experienced on Earth. One must react to problems in a physical way. This is a shift of movement to develop the manifestation of unseen help from angels. This is the defined culmination of thought and determination.

An action toward a goal is noticed and ways are put in action toward its achievement. Action is an undertaking of thought through the senses, which is the mortal way. To move into the actuality of a thought, you must take action toward its manifestation. Thought alone rarely can bring the reality of development to the soul.

Earth is made up of embodied souls. Physical exertion is part of Earth. If souls desire to wait until thought alone brings it, they may wait a long time. Thought is good but use the senses and physical exertion to attain what is desired.

Lift the Quality of Thought

How can we help humanity through prayer?

The mass of intellect on Earth will override the ignorance of lesser souls. To achieve this, each soul must be worthy of self-love. Each must be able to send love through thought communication. Each must be able to lift the quality of thought to communicate with beings of heavenly scope. The world is in a tender state. There must be intelligence on Earth.

The world must now be given the words of angels. Each soul of Earth is to evolve within itself to be the most wonderful and most intelligent soul possible. It is neither necessary to recall the past nor to ask forgiveness or repentance for things of the past. This moment, this second, is all. If a soul has killed a thousand bodies and now asks for help in lifting from ignorance, it will be given. Humanity's punishment and justice is not the justice dispensed by God.

Intellect begins the self-journey to lift you to your highest being. The level of ignorance on Earth will remain. The world will continue sinking into wars, despondency, evilness, and pain. But this can still be avoided.

Each soul begins a prayer to God asking for help to be lifted from the world, from this. To be lifted to the angels and to the one great God, only a desire is needed. Ask with a sincere heart. The angels know the sincerity of your soul. The angels know the love, the fears — all that is you. If each soul asked for help, all the intelligence in all the heavens in all the worlds would rush to Earth. Miracles of great multitudes would occur. People's thoughts are of varied levels lingering in the atmosphere of Earth. If the lower levels ceased to exist and the higher levels of thought permeated Earth, what wonders would occur! The wonders of the heavens might be seen on Earth.

Lift the quality of thought. The creation of love can be cultivated in the mind. Send this love to another being. To do this, feel love with all emotion. Focus this love on another. The mind thinks of the happiness of the self. To put this welfare of another before oneself, even in a small way, is a way of giving love to another. The most important reason for doing this is, of course, the soul's growth but also the preservation of humanity.

Write to God

How do we write to God or the angels?

Writing to an angel is a way of understanding and focusing thoughts. Angels read and understand. When a thought force is undefined and illusive, the thought will be stronger and more defined. We read words with you and try to help you in any way.

When you write a letter to God, write the purpose of the letter, why it is so urgent, and ask humbly for God's direction. God is planning at all times and can intervene any action at any stage. God will honor requests made with the deepest desire of the soul if they are requested with a humble heart. God will judge the worth of the request. If it is not necessary for the soul, it will not be attained.

Live now! Live today! All desires will not be attained this day. When the time is preplanned for this attainment, the soul must wait. With the most sacred, most sincere prayer, God will decide when it is to be granted. People can only know in a limited way. God knows the changes that will occur on Earth.

An angel overlooking another can be called to you. It is accomplished as requested. Whoever is asked will come forth to receive messages. We are to bring wellness and compassion to souls. Angels can help relations with others by guiding souls to open their hearts to love. We must let people decide their own destinies, but we can help if it is God's will.

Feelings are the most important communications in the universe. When you speak your feelings, the angels listen and feel your emotions. Choose words most carefully. When thoughts are directed to God, the heart's sincerity is known by the angels. When words are spoken to God, the heart's sincerity is known by the angels. When words are spoken to God, let them not be hollow words. Feelings are the true words of God. We are the words and the feelings.

Ask God, who is all-knowing, if this is the best action for all at this time. God gives more than anyone can know. A seemingly insignificant desire in your eyes could change all plans for the future — not only for you, but also for all humankind. Do not write what you desire without concern over effects that could occur. Write only with a full understanding of all consequences of an action. Every wish has covenants.

You can talk to us if you see us. You may ask God to send his holy angels to protect you and teach you to be a better person. A world with angelic intervention is most blessed in the universe. When you ask God to send an angel protector to you, you will be answered in an instant. Angels will surround you and guard your words and actions. When this occurs, all your actions are in harmony with the workings of God. We will be with anyone who asks.

Can writing to angels bring us our desires?

We see what is written and read your thoughts. We understand the deepest desires. Ask questions specifically. We will read and understand them. Prayer or writing takes the thoughts and makes them specific. When this is done, the thoughts are formulated into specific desires. If the mind can picture the thought in all detail, it makes way for the desire to be real. Write to the angels by sitting and writing with a pen or other writing instrument. Ask the angels for help in whatever is needed.

The angels see the words written and understand this is concentrated, directed thought. This is not like the thoughts in the mind that may be fleeting and difficult to interpret. This is understood and discussed with the angels. This is not a prayer, as prayers are to be directed to God, the Father in heaven. When requests are read, the angels also hear your thoughts. This is more clearly accepted than unfocused thoughts or random conversation.

How can we get our prayers answered?

The way to have things you desire is to ask for them through the method of prayer. When you have a desire, you tend to ask God for it, but you must also make the way clear for it to come to you. The way to do this is to mention the ways it can be obtained. A path will be cleared between you and the desire so that it can come to you. It will come, not by alteration of movement, but by attraction. Make no barriers between you and the desire. Make it easy to obtain by attracting it to you. Meet it with expectancy. The desire will now be yours.

Any number of requests and prayers can be placed before God, the Father. We feel that a good prayer wants nothing but to praise God and give thanks for all giving. We want to make most clear: Be careful of the wish, and keep the desire that no one be hurt or harmed in any way. This is most important!

You are to give your own thoughts to God, in your own way. A prepared speech is not the best way to talk to God. Simply waiting until your heart lets go of pain and anger is best. Talk to him in your own way. A sincere soul reaches God better than the most finely worded prayer. Prayer is speaking to God through the soul. Many wonder if prayers are heard. The answer is yes.

Prayer alone — speaking from the heart — will bring love and joy into your life. You must be thankful for what you have willed. When you will an object, and it is yours, thank the power of the heavens for helping you receive it. Your food is a part of this. All things are energy particles created by thought. Be thankful for the things you have received. We angels will try to help those who lift their thoughts to God. Many pray to have things given to them. These are not the most desirable prayers to send God. God hears all thoughts and prayers.

All prayers are given answers in your life span. A way to meet your desires may be given by the angels if it is desired. Listening to us in your mind will let you know if it is to be. We weld our minds to yours. This will be the answer you can expect to receive. We hear prayers to extend life. We weigh the responsibilities on Earth and the glories of heaven. We decide the necessary outcome. God overlooks all lives on Earth.

Put Feeling and Focus in Prayers

Why do so many prayers seem to be ineffective?

When praying, you cannot say the words without feeling, nor can you mention names of people you do not know because you have no specific feelings toward them. These words, used in prayer, will not effect change. Prayer must be felt in the soul. This is not to say words given aloud are not given credence, but words alone have no worth or power if not accompanied by feeling. This is so important.

To strengthen your mental thoughts, you would be wise to write your desires on paper. Read the desires repeatedly. Open the heart and mind to receiving these desires. The way to strengthen the mind is to think the thought as intensely as possible without speaking it aloud. This may take a long time to accomplish, as the mind will need to be retrained. The mind is accustomed to weak, undirected thought. In prayer, it is being introduced to strong, directed thought. Focus your thought on a person. Repeat this many times. The thought will be received.

When this is accomplished, the thought will be powerful. This thought must be directed to those in need. You should desire their needs and picture them in wonderful circumstances. As you use this technique, you will become more and more proficient. As this multiplies, more and more people will begin to help those in need through thought. This can be done.

This will help others in a way never conceived before. This will prepare the mind for entrance into the higher spheres. Life will be enhanced. The repercussions of this power will be felt everywhere. Do this not to obtain things for yourself but to help others. Think of another soul in need this day. More goodness begins with thoughts of others than thoughts of yourself. A prayer for another is watched and recorded by the angels. It is heard and called into conference. A most sincere prayer gives more to others than one can possibly know.

You will be made to see the ways you can help the needy through thought. One way is to desire their needs be fulfilled. Think of food entering the bodies of the hungry. Plan it in your thoughts. It will occur as you desire. These thoughts were given to you to use as you desire. The power of these thoughts has not yet been utilized on Earth. Thoughts must be directed by picturing the recipient. When these thoughts are directed to this person, they are felt in the soul immediately. The stronger the thought, the more deeply it is felt.

You may wish to help someone who is in pain or is suffering. You should think of this person as healthy and well. Directing strong thoughts can accomplish wonderful healing. When the way you love is opened to the entire world, we will tell you the important ways to help. Most importantly, weld with the angels around you. Make a world of wonders with your desires. Open the love inside. To let go of the love, direct it toward those who need it most. Help the people around you by sending focused love. It will help humanity.

We want the plan to be fulfilled. We will guide you in this way. Make each hour a new discovery. Make each moment greater in varied ways. Love is the way we express many key responses to the world. When angels are close, try to feel the love we send to you.

What has happened when you prayed for someone to live but the person still died?

The will of God supersedes the will of mortals. This soul may be needed in another place. Its work on Earth may have been fulfilled. Many factors affect this outcome. The basic plan of life is not without pains. Would you want the soul to remain in the diseased body? Many times the prayer will not help to keep the soul on Earth but, in sending love, it helps make the soul's lifting easier.

It is true that prayer can heal the body and raise the deceased again in a body, but those on Earth are to let the soul lift to God if this is decreed. The ways of God are not always understood by humanity.

How do angels feel when they hear, or "overhear," prayers?

When children lift their heads in prayer, we wait to hear their sincerity. Adults now pray in unison, in repetition, and in words without meaning. The feelings are hums. There is no opening of the soul, no chasm of the heart. Oh, how the light emanates from the soul's heart!

Let the emotions come forth to us. All can be bared to us angels of God. We do not judge any action. We will do whatever we can to help you, but we must know your sincerity. You may bear your burdens to God. Create your words from your feelings, not by mimicking phrases.

The Soul Is All Perception

How can we feel the soul?

Each moment on Earth is to be cherished. Feel gratitude, for the moments rejoice in the wonders of the world. The moments in nature are to be treasured. Enjoy the world as it is now, even though it is wrought with pain and suffering. This is the place you are now experiencing. This is to be viewed not with sadness but with wonderment. Each moment can be perceived in a variety of ways. Choose beneficial ways of expression.

The workings of the mind are delicate. Perception changes because of the many factors. Let the soul feel freedom from the containment of the body. The soul lifts during deep sleep. The soul may lift through prayer or in moments of quietness. The soul is the infinite you. The soul is all perception. Revere the soul within. The peacefulness resounds within.

All wisdom, all intelligence, resides in the soul. Let the soul lift to the surface of your thoughts enjoy freedom and bring qualities of the infinite into the mind. The soul is the self. This is what is viewed by the angels and all heavenly creatures. This is a wonder of God within humanity.

How does the average person supersede the masses to become truly and sincerely spiritual in a practical way?

We are always with you, even if we see you from the heavens. We can appear in many places. Much of the time, we are beside or about you. When chaos, discordant sounds or actions, demands, and yelling occur, or when anger is shown or harbored in the mind, these things will not bring us to you. Cleanse the body and mind. Speak in softness. Let the purity of the soul shine forth.

Let care show in the abode, the surroundings, the food, the body — all. When all is readied and prepared, ask us to come and be with you. We will enter and stand beside you. This is a time to kneel in private and pay homage to God. We will carry the prayer to God.

The way to do the sacred rite is not to speak aloud when addressing the Holy Spirit. When addressing the great God of all — or Abraham or Jesus — call the name aloud in bravery and boldness. Immediately humble your person by kneeling before the one you address and bowing your head in submission.

Cleanse the body. Dress in dignity and cleanliness. Speak from the feelings deep in your heart. Confess all thought and deed not of rightness. You may give fruit and flowers as an offering. Ask to be lifted from ignorance and human frailty into the opening of your heart. Give sincere thankfulness from the deepness of your heart.

Govern the self throughout all endeavors. Your prayers are to be given with devotion and a righteous heart. Your conduct will be close to God. You will be aware at all times of the understanding of the guardian angels. The wonder of this is the welding between you and the entities of the highest. This work is to be done to receive the miracles of the heavenly entities.

This is a way of devotion to the one God. Wonders will occur in a life prepared and expectant. The joys reaped from this endeavor will lift the soul toward God.

Integral Prayer

Can you describe another way to pray?

One way you use prayer is through verbal communication and a second way is through silent thought. Another way to pray is called "integral prayer." This third way is done by welding with angels. This is accomplished by complete relaxation and asking the angels to merge with you so that you can comprehend all their thoughts and feelings. It takes much time to integrate. You should fall into a meditation or almost a sleep. Make the request and experience the angels merging. This can be done when one has time to experience it, as it is not done swiftly.

Integral prayer is another way to reach God. It is not done through action. Rather, it is done in quietness, solitude, and humbleness. This prayer is more difficult, as it takes preparation to pull oneself into a state of respectfulness and reverence. This is a method of closeness with the heavenly angels. It is a total relaxation of the body and mind into a meditative state, then a realization of the state and communion with the heavenly entities.

What wonders can occur from this prayer! One may have visions of the future or know people's thoughts. Many truths are revealed if this is done repetitiously and in great reverence. Integral prayer is a way of communing with the gods and the angels. Even the most lowly souls of Earth can do this.

- Sit.
- Let the mind relax as if sleep were coming.
- Ask the angels to weld with you as your mind delves deeper and deeper into the pure essence of the soul.
- Ask for what you desire with a most humble heart.

The body will be a vessel to enact the powers of the gods and angels.

Let this be replicated once or twice daily, if possible. This prayer will evoke many truths and wonders.

This is the most sacred of all the types of prayer to God. This takes discipline and the giving of oneself. The measure of the soul is brought forth for the viewing of the gods. The sacredness of this communion will be noted by all heavenly beings. The moments of welding with the higher entities are to be cherished. This is a most sacred growth of the soul.

When the prayer is finished, arise and give thanks.

Connecting with God

If someone has a desperate need, how can that person really connect with God?

Ask God what you need in the most profound way. The most honorable way to do this is to bless all in the heavens and bless all the angels around you with sincere prayer. Make this request after the body has detached from the soul, if possible. This is done by separation, either in deep sleep — when the soul does not need the body — in deep meditation, or by fasting. This is a preparation for prayer.

The prayer should be given when you are alone and after you have cleansed the body. The prayer should be done in an uncluttered place. It should be clean and without malice. The area should be prepared for the entrance of God. Homage of fruit and flowers may be offered as a gift.

As you request mercy, you must hold the sanctity of a pure heart and a sweetness of the soul. Open your heart so that God and the angels can see the light, the energy, and the softness of your soul. Bring this to consecration. Your prayer should be given in the most humble manner. Wear simple, clean clothing, and leave your feet bare. Let go of any fear, animosity, hate, or malice.

You are requesting an audience from the most high in the heavens. This is an honor not bestowed on all mortals. Nothing stands between you and your God now.

- Behave as if you can see God, as if he is standing before you.
- Drop to your knees, if possible.
- Drop your head.
- Give him honor worthy of his greatness.

- Give your thanks so that it may be seen in your heart.
- Ask your question sincerely and humbly, not in the form of words from the mouth but from a pure heart and deep soul.
- Thank the one God with the same feeling.
- Arise. Question no more.

God has heard your prayer. Your home has been filled with the angels of God, with the gods of the heavens, and with the light of God, as well as the light of Jesus, Abraham, Japheth, and the gods who wish to hear your plea.

Know that if the gods give appointment to the query and all is ordained, the gift will be given from the heavens. Know within that this will be done. You have agreed to all the covenants. This means you will now accept conditions; should the way to acquire this gift be encumbered with ways not clear, the repercussions will be held by you.

Take great care before the request is made. Think the words as clearly as possible before the request. Hold this honor in great esteem. God sees into the soul of the body. This must be given with a true and loyal heart. People of wisdom will abide the love of God. Ignorant people will vary according to their whims. This is a secret of the most sacred. Let this not be a whimsical variant.

This is the most sacred covenant between your soul and all the powers in the heavens. Do not take this lightly. If an angel appears to give direction, follow the directions as told. If an angel does not appear but comes in a dream or vision, give this the same worth. Be aware of the promptings from the angel's whisperings, for they can lead you to your desire.

This will be fulfilled. Thank God for the fulfillment, for one day you will stand before him and give homage to him and to the gods. We now have given you a most sacred way to meet your desires.

Prayer Guide

Prayer

We wish to tell you of prayer.
We are to say the communication between God and humanity
is a most sacred interaction. This is given in all solemnity.
It is not to be given lightly.

Does God Exist?

When the soul lifts to see the light of God before it,
the feelings of joy are so immense, the soul trembles,
not from fear but from ecstasy.
This is more reality than the life now lived,
which is in the fog of misunderstanding.

The bliss is so that the soul falls at the feet of God
to bear the thankfulness of the moment.
The soul gasps in awe. This is the most culminating
moment in eternity. A soul remembers this throughout
all lives and all experiences.

To have audience with the one God is not explainable
in the words of Earth. This is more concrete than any experience.
This is the view, the thought, the scent, the music,
the light, the feeling, the love of the absolute
finest spectrum of all existence.

The first thought of a human being is:
"Am I worthy of this?"
No matter what has happened in the past,
the soul is exalted in the heavens.
Love supersedes all.
The intensity of love fills the soul beyond expression.

To view God is the exaltation of the soul.
The sight of God will lift the heart of the soul
to extreme tenderness and blissfulness.

One on Earth, even in extreme imagination,
cannot fathom the emotion one feels
in the presence of the one God.
This is the most extreme love the soul can feel.
The emanation of the one God is more than can be comprehended.

The Holy Spirit

The Holy Spirit is all light and vapor. He is masculine in nature.
All love emanates in this light.
This is beyond any feeling known by mortals.
This is the finest spectrum of existence.
As one becomes finer and finer, lighter and lighter,
the most tender feelings are deciphered.

One cannot see the Holy Spirit. One cannot touch the Holy Spirit.
One can't even speak aloud to the Holy Spirit.
Even the thought of humans is too course to communicate.

When addressing the Holy Spirit,
one is not to use words aloud, as they are too coarse for the finest
spectrum of thought. One is to use the most gentle thought
        in the softest message possible.
He is a specter of all thought and energy.
The Holy Spirit will not answer prayers given.
The souls of Earth can't receive communication with this
sacred God, nor can a soul of Earth look upon this sacred God,
as it would blind the eyes.

God's angels, archangels, and heavenly entities may at times
reveal thought to this Holy Spirit.
Whereas the one God may appear in the physical, the Holy Spirit
        will not.
The Holy Spirit is not to be begged or pleaded with as God.
No prayers are to be directed to him,
as the coarseness would repel his magnificence.

He is all-powerful, all love, in all ways.
He is a being of more beauty than all beings.

One may bless the Holy Spirit, but only with bowed head
and closed eyes. This may be done only with the softest thought.
A human shall not ever gaze upon this entity.
To feel his power, one must be in the heavens.

The immensity of love can't be explained in any words on Earth.
The Holy Spirit is a more exalted being than can be expressed.
Picture in the mind a spirit so intensely beautiful,
you can't even raise your head to view it, can't look upon it,
can't open your ears to hear it.

A mortal man will never be in audience with this entity.
The thought of mortals is too brazen to be received
by this entity, even in the most delicate of prayer or the most
tender love one can feel.

Know of his existence. This is enough for the mortals of Earth.
The Holy Spirit is beyond the comprehension of mortals.

Does God Hear Our Prayers?

God exists.
We now need to let all know God hears prayer.
God will designate which prayers are to be answered
    in a positive manner.
The force of thought is a necessary movement in
the act of sending a prayer to God.

Don't ever think you are just talking to yourself
or that your thoughts, your pleas, your prayers,
go unnoticed. They now seem to be in a wanting
phase to increase material possessions.
A prayer for another is given much worth.

The Address

The way the sacred rite is done is this:
When addressing the Holy Spirit,
do not speak aloud.

When addressing the great God of all
    or Abraham or Jesus,
call the name aloud in bravery and boldness.
Immediately humble your person by kneeling
before him and bowing your head in submission.

Preparation for Prayer

To give words or sounds without feeling the prayer is surface.
It gives no worth to the words.
Most don't spend even a moment in the happiness of others.
To enhance the quality of life for anyone other than oneself
    is a loving, giving act of selflessness.
This is viewed by angels and gods alike.
Let the soul lift at one's own pace. This can't be forced.

The prayers are to be given singularly unless the group as
    individuals feel deeply the prayer's purpose.
No performances of prayers are to be viewed,
as attention is to be retained by the self instead of the direct
    purpose.
The body is to be at ease.
No urgency, panic, or fear is to be felt when addressing the one
    God.
The more calm and gentle the prayer, the better.
The demeanor is to be the softest calmness of the mind.
The thought is to be clear and unfettered.
It's not necessary to verbalize a prayer for the one God.
All angels and all gods can understand the thought as well as
the sincerity of the emotion. To enact perfected homage,
the head is bowed, if possible.
This often can't be performed because of the body.
This is to be given with all humbleness for God in all intelligence,
    all creation, and all glory.

Human thought is fragmented and scattered. It's important to ask

with the notion in direct, clear thought.
The mind must be understood. This is difficult when thought
banters into many varied options.

The most important part of the prayer is the sincerity.
This must be felt in the soul, as sounds mouthed give no credence
to the prayer. The prayer must be felt in the soul.

Direct your prayer to your derivatives of God, for under
      many names is the true, sacred, holy one God.
Even though some prayers are directed to the holy angels to fulfill,
They are not to be directed to the angels, to any other gods,
or to any other entities on any worlds or in any heavens.
This sacred communication is between your soul and God alone.

Cleanse the body and mind if possible.
Let the purity of the soul shine forth.
If it is possible, let care show in the surroundings, the abode,
      the food, the body — all.
We will enter and stand behind you.
This is a time to kneel in private and pay homage to God.
The cleanliness is appreciated and the care given to surroundings
      shows the quality of the soul.
One should try to be in a respectful manner, but God hears all
      prayers.
It's not necessary to have fine arraignments nor to be in all
      cleanliness.

Prayers are given and received, for God sees the soul that is you.
He hears your soul. This is what truly matters.

We angels will carry the prayer to God.
If possible, dress in dignity and cleanliness.

Speak with feelings deep in the heart.
Confess all thought and deeds not of rightness.

Ask God to lift you from ignorance and human frailty.
Give sincere thankfulness.

Govern the self throughout all endeavors.
The prayers are to be given with devotion and a righteous heart.
Your conduct will be close to God.
You will be aware at all times of the understanding of the angels.
The wonder of this is the welding between you and the entities
    of the highest.
This is a way of the devotion to the one God.
Wonders will occur in a life prepared and expectant.
The joys reaped from this endeavor will lift the soul before God.

Directing Prayer

The prayer is always given only to God.
The most sincere, genuine, heartfelt prayer
    is given much worth.

This can be addressed as you desire.
"Dear God" or "Heavenly Father"
is a wonderful address,
as long as you know the prayer is addressed to God.
This may be a prayer of words, thoughts, or feelings.

The angels hear the prayers and know the thoughts
of humankind. We know the sincerity.
The prayer may be given to us by God
to enact or discuss; but pray not to us.
Pray to God in the heavens.

How to Pray

Feel the empathy in your own heart.
Every experience opens the heart to feel.
Clothe yourself in all humility, for you are giving homage and
    humbleness before God.
Bow or kneel, as you are not speaking to a peer.
This is the almighty God of all.
This is to be done in solitude if possible,
because the thought and verbiage are clear and unfettered.
The focus is on the one God.

The calmness is to be mentioned.
The sanctity of the soul is to be revealed to God alone.
Give the strongest thought possible.
Give the most organized thought possible.
Give the greatest sincerity possible.
Give the deepest gratitude possible.
This is a direct communication with the one holy God
    of all in all spheres.
Don't give this lightly.
This is the most intense communication possible.
Pray as if you were standing before God.
The most magnificent brilliance is before you.
The soul will tremble, and you will fall to your knees.
What words will befall the mind?
What emotions will be felt?

Give clarity and strength to the thought.
Give love encased in the soul to God.
Give thanks for things not yet received to God.

Ask the prayer or plea.
Give thanks.
Hold thankfulness in your heart during the performance of the
    prayer.
Don't ever think this isn't heard
    or given to the one God.
One may wait a long time for the deliverance of the prayer
    or it may be given at once.

This is determined by the one God, the angels,
the plans of others, the destiny of the country and the world,
the force of thought, the clarity of thought, and the sense of feeling.

This cannot be obtained without the feelings of the soul.

The Answering of Prayers

The meeting of angels are to place the directives from God
in the proper order of importance.
We discuss how to best handle the prayers.

The seemingly most insignificant prayer can have the
highest power in these decisions.
The angels discuss all aspects of a decision.
If the mortals of Earth wish to make a plea before angels,
they are to pray to God.
This is a most valued decision.
The angels weigh each possibility.

When a decision is made, the angel in charge of the soul
will enact the decision. The souls of Earth are not to question
the decisions of God or his appointed angels.

If it is decreed that a mass of souls must lift from Earth,
let it be known it's for a reason not understood
      by the souls of Earth.
All these souls may be needed in another place at this time.
The souls are not in sorrow. The souls are in blissfulness.
If it seems this is not the way one should desire,
it is known by God and his holy angels.
They are not a mention of the people of Earth.
Consider it may change all destinies to lift these souls.
All movements of souls, Earth, and all things are because God
in heaven has decreed these movements
for purposes not understood by humans.

The directive from God is all.
This is the word.
This is to be carried out by the angels.

We are with a most loving God.
God is powerful and merciful.
God is all.
We are honored to be the most sacred angels of God.
This is to be with all souls.
The word of God is a wonder to be treasured.
It is an honor to hear his word.

Deciding the Answers to Prayers

Pray to God with thankfulness in your heart.
Compose your message to God as if you were writing a letter.
You are not to manipulate.
You are not to covet.
You aren't to follow or parrot others or to
give the names of the gods and angels frivolously in requests.

Are you uttering phrases of no meaning?
Speak from the heart of the soul.
It's not necessary to use lovely language.
God understands all pleas.
He understands all feelings.
Even the most simple plea will be lifted to God because
of the sincerity with which it was given.

The most sincere prayer will be given to God before all others.
God has given the holy angels dominion over the answering of
    prayers.
God has sanctified us to answer as he overlooks.
We meet to discuss the prayers and pleas.
Of all pleas projected with love for God,
we can reach to weld with the soul.

If the plea is from fear, desperation, panic, anger, or pain, it's more
    difficult to infiltrate the heart of the soul.
Guidance will always be given to our charges on Earth.
If you understood how important prayer on Earth is to God,
you would be in continuous homage to God for all life on Earth.
Every moment would be given to incessant prayer.

Can one even do this?
No, this is not a feasible method of praise.
Give instead the pleas and prayers with force,
with a torque of power from your mind and soul.

A mention of prayer can be a powerful method of attainment
of any desire. The prayer is given flight to the realm of angels.
It's sorted for importance and answered.
All pleas mentally directed to God are given to God.
All prayers directed to Jesus are given to Jesus.
We are the emissaries to radiate the purpose on Earth.
God has given directives for us to determine the importance of
    prayer.

Desires

When you want the desire, you ask God for it, but you must make
the way clear for it to come to you.
The way to do this is to mention the ways this can be obtained.
A path will be cleared between you and the desire, so it
may come to you.
It will come not by alteration of movement but by attraction.
Make no barriers between you and the desire.
Make it easy to obtain by attracting it to you.
Meet it with expectancy.
The desire will now be yours.

Any number of requests and prayers can be placed before God.
A good prayer wants nothing but to praise God and give thanks
for all giving.

We want to make most clear:
Be careful of the wish. Hold the desire that no one be hurt
or harmed in any way. This is most important.

Each man is to give his own thoughts to God in his own way.
A prepared speech is not the best way to talk to God.
A simple waiting until your heart lets go of the pain and anger
would be best.
Talk to God in your own way. A sincere soul reaches God more
than the most finely worded prayer.
Prayer is speaking to God from the soul.
Prayer alone, speaking from the heart, will bring joy
and love into the life.
You must be thankful for what you will.

When you will an object and it has become yours,
thank the power of the heavens for helping you receive it.
Your food is part of this.
Be thankful for gifts received.
We angels try to help the one who lifts his thoughts to God.
Many pray to have things given to them.
These are not the most desirable prayers.
Know that God hears all thoughts and prayers.

Prayers are given answers in the life span of man.
A man listening to us in his mind will know if it is to be.
We weld our mind to yours.

We hear prayers to extend life.
We weigh the responsibilities on Earth and the glories of heaven.
From this we decide the necessary outcome.

Factors in the Answering of Prayers

The reason prayers are answered for one person and not another is:
the sincerity,
the life plan,
the movements of the elements,
the strength of thought,
the power of the forces of the soul's openness to God, and
the growth development of the soul.
All these factors play parts in the outcome.

The Opening of the Heart

The opening of the heart begins through prayer.
Directed thought with sincere feeling will open
the soul's irregular movement. This vibration
or movement in the soul will let tenderness into
the heart and mind.

The tenderness is a giving of oneself to God.
The surrender of the self will give way to
understanding the spiritual realm.
Giving sincere thankfulness will also open
the heart to feeling. The beauty of the soul will
permeate the mind and physical body to bring
a peacefulness and gentleness to the energy
    of the person.

Once this has been opened, the way to God is found.
There is a deepening of emotion, an aliveness in the body,
a lifting of the spirit. There is a remembrance of the
    aliveness of the soul in the heavens.
A child has this remembrance, but the soul loses this most
    precious joyousness over time.
To enact this again in a human life is a wonderful feeling.

To touch the core of the soul within and let it rise to the daily
    activities affects all surroundings.
Let the actions of the body not be from a hollow nucleus.
Let the actions come from the integration
    of the soul and mind.

This will bring a softness and aliveness to life.
A thankfulness, a wonder, and a most tender heart will be sustained
in daily activities.
Let the soul open and be vulnerable to the world.
The soul is always protected.

Feelings

In prayer, the words are less important than the feelings.
The ways to God are revealed through prayer.

The thought is clarified during a prayer.
This engages the mind to focus.
This is the beginning of the strong thought needed to help others.

Prayer is a plea or thanksgiving to God.
This opens the heart to express feelings. Feeling is necessary for the
growth of the soul.

Prayer helps you decide what is most important to you.
This helps organize your thoughts and priorities.

You are addressing God. This is not a menial address.
You are opening your heart to not only God but to all the gods
and angels in the heavens. Your feelings, words, and thoughts
are of great importance.

Prayer integrates your body with your soul.
This integration is necessary for the growth of the soul.
It lifts your level of consciousness to an area of communication and
welding with angelic forces and with God.
The act of prayer is submission to a greater force than oneself.
This begins a path of growth only found in submission to God.

Emotions are integral. Feeling empathy and compassion for any
other soul besides oneself and pleading for that soul with sincerity
and a depth of feeling,

This is watched by the gods.
This is noted and a profound greatness is placed on the soul.
The opening holds compassion to the point of tears,
an empathy for all living souls,
a gentleness and tenderness of more softness
    than one can endure.

The human soul is filled with beauty unimaginable.
One must open this for growth toward God.
This can be achieved through prayer to God,
giving all servitude to the great God.

A plea to God for anyone other than oneself will open the chasms
    of love encased in the soul.
The enormity of this is not to be found because
it goes on into eternity, developing more
and more with every lifetime.
Love deepens and grows during life.
It expands during life unless constantly thwarted.

May your prayers reflect the beauty of your soul.
When we speak of you, we speak of the soul that is you.

You are seen in all places as a soul of light.
The brightness of the light will show the evolution
    of the soul.
When one is engaged in a prayer of gratitude, of thankfulness
deeply felt, this is seen by the gods and angels.
This is not to be said without feeling,
for it will have no meaning.

If you think of something for which you are sincerely
thankful, give thanks to God for this.
Angels will bend to hear the words and thoughts
    given to God.
This is the most beautiful prayer one can give.

God receives all prayers and will overjoy at your giving.
Let all feelings pour into the prayer.
Thankfulness opens the heart to be with the angels of God.
This is given as the angels of God on Earth will be heard
    by all people.

When one's heart opens to receive thought from angels,
it also opens to receive gifts from worlds beyond Earth.
All things are manifested first in thought,
    then in physical manifestation on Earth.

This is a merging of the heavenly entities.
This is done neither through fear nor anger but through the
    development of love and thankfulness for all given.
If it be felt to the point of tenderness of the soul's heart and
the trembling of the soul, be assured,
God is listening.

Action in the Fulfillment of Desire

An exertion is necessary for those on Earth to create
circumstances where exception is necessary.
Miracles can be attained but only in circumstances
    where exception is necessary.
Lift to God in your thought and prayer,
    but walk Earth.
The physical body is here to use.

Action is necessary.
All time can be spent in thought, but if not acted on,
    it is not valid in reality.
When the most important goals are your words and thought,
use the action of the physical to enact the desire.
The mention of the physical is not abhorrent to angels.
Earth is a physical world.
To weep and wail or plead and pray are ways of achieving
    but take much time and energy.
Asking the divine can bring achievement, but taking your own
    physical action to achieve a goal is a much used way on Earth.

Many wonder how to achieve specific goals.
The ways are known.
Take an action most in alignment with the ways of God.
Earth is in alignment with physical action.
Bring the physical action to the fore and use it
    for the most good.

The senses of man and the physical presence of the human body
give the thought and feelings of a method of enactment.

Were one able to use only thought,
one would not have been born on this lowly Earth.
The body is to be used in the achievement of
the mind's desires. Bring the desires to fruition
through the combination of thought from the mind,
feelings from the heart and the senses, and
exertion from the physical body.

The more the integration is developed, the more
    benefits are accrued.
Live not only in the mind and heart but in the body's physical
    action as well.
The most welcome influences come from taking action.
Often the thoughts are so vague as to not be
    acknowledged by unseen forces.
An action can be seen and felt.
These entities join your energies to help bring the desire.

Action is the gross manifestation of thought.
The performance of action in a physical way is a
manifestation of thought. In a positive manner,
this always brings a flood of repercussions in seen
    and unseen ways.
The physical manifestation is what is experienced on Earth.
One must react to problems in a physical way.
This is a shift of movement to develop the manifestation of
    unseen help from angels.

This is the defined culmination of thought and determination.
An action taken toward a goal is noticed, and the ways are put in
    action to the achievement.
Action is an undertaking of the thought through the senses,
    which is the mortal way.
To move into the actuality of the thought, one must take action
    toward its manifestation.
Thought alone rarely can bring

the reality of development to the soul.

Earth is made up of embodied souls. Physical exertion is
 part of Earth.
If souls desire to wait until thought alone brings it,
 they may wait a long time.
Thought is good, but use the senses and physical exertion
 to attain what is desired.

Writing a Letter to God

When you write to God, state the purpose of the letter,
   why it is so urgent, and ask humbly for God's direction.

God is planning at all times and can intervene any action at any
   stage.
God will honor requests made with the deepest desire of the soul
   if they are requested with a humble heart.
God will judge the worth of the request.

When thoughts are directed to God or when words are spoken to
   God,
the heart's sincerity is known by the angels. Let the words not be
   hollow.

Feelings are the true words of God.
We are the words and the feelings.
Feelings are the most important communications in the universe.
When you speak your feelings, the angels listen and feel the
   emotions.
Choose your words carefully.

A person may ask God to send his holy angels to protect him and
   teach him to be a better man.
A man with angelic intervention is most blessed in the universe.
A man asking God to send an angel protector to him will be
   answered in an instant.
Angels will surround the man and guard his words and actions.
When this occurs, all his actions are in harmony with
   the workings of God.

Angels will be with anyone who asks.

Writing to God or to the angels becomes a way of understanding
and focusing your thoughts.
Angels read and understand.
When a thought force is undefined and illusive, this will make the
thoughts stronger and more defined.
The angels read the words with you and try to help in any way.
When this is done, the thoughts are formulated into specific
desires.
If the mind can picture the thought in all detail, it makes way for
the thought to become real.
Angels see what is written and read the thoughts of man.
We understand the deepest desires.
Ask questions specifically. Angels will read and understand.
Written prayer takes the thoughts and makes them specific.

This is concentrated, directed thought. This is not like a mood,
which may be fleeting, unfocused, and difficult to interpret.
This is understood and discussed among the angels.
When requests are read, the angels also hear your thoughts.
They are more clearly accepted than random thought or
conversation.

Ask the all-knowing God the best action for all at this time.
God gives more than anyone may know.
A seemingly insignificant desire, in your eyes, may change all plans
for the future,
not only for you but for all humanity.
Don't write what you desire without concern over effects that
could occur.
Write only with a full understanding of all consequences
of an action.
Every wish has covenants.

No one can be hurt from this action.

The way must be made clear for receiving the desire.
A request may be made in detail, but one must not
tell the angels how to make this come about.

The living material result of a desire must be open to
    manifestation.
This must be clear.
The workings of all other plans of manifestation must be in
    agreement with the result of this request.

Write the desire on paper. Read this many times.
Think about this desire.
Feel that this desire has already happened. Feel this!
Simulate how you will feel when this desire comes into reality.
Let this happiness surround you.

The human mind is capable of achieving greatness.
Feel the movement of the achievement of the desire into reality.
Know this can be attained!

Visualizing

Feel the way you will be when your prayer is received.
Picturing this in your mind will help bring the desired results.
You can plead and pray, but until it is known in the mind,
that it will be present in all feeling and experiences as if it's already
    occurred,
the prayer is not accepted by the mind.

It may still happen, but you are to trust this will occur to
enact specific results.

Meditation

Meditation can bring levels of consciousness through the
    processes of experiencing the soul within.
Prayer is more widespread, and the holiness of the soul can be felt
through the awareness of God, the angels, and all entities of the
    heavens,
but is only a method if indulged regularly.

One is an external plea.
The other is an internal fusing of the self.
A use of the physical body is necessary for the meditation
    and will clearly bring one to God.
Prayer is external and holds a deep infusion of the belief
    that God hears and will respond.

Can one do both?
Yes, the usage of both techniques in life bonds with the self
    and with God.
This develops the growth of the soul in maximum proficiency.

One may stand alone and grow little if desired.
One may meditate and grow in the development of consciousness.
One may exaggerate the wisdom, the compassion, the tenderness,
    and the love to bring into focused prayer.

This lifts the curtain of self-attainment to let the luminous soul
    be known in all worlds and all heavens.
Both are seen to be ways of development toward God.

The movements are much the same in that they both lift the soul
    to deeper attainments.
The latter, prayer, is the supreme acknowledgement
of not only the existence of God, but the complete giving of one's
    life to God.

In deep meditation or in deep prayer, the great chasm of the intense
    soul is felt.
One is to not speak to God from a level of only the body.
One must communicate from the enduring soul.
Meditation is a technique to feel the soul and bring out the qualities
    of the soul to the exterior life on Earth.
Prayer is a movement of desiring to be one with God.
A deepening of values occurs with each technique.
The movement of the angels occurs only through prayer.
A unification of the thinking and the action occurs through both.
The deliberate desire to be closer to God occurs in both.
A life of deepened values, purity of thought, and the seeking of
    God's presence into the life is present in both.

When a moment of the soul is discovered,
    the soul opens to receive God.
The moment is received in a trembling, a gasping,
    a fluttering, a gentle lifting.
To experience the soul is as if you were watching a butterfly
    move from a cocoon.
You are becoming a beautiful creature of God.
You are your soul.
This experience is of the self, not of any group action.
The love within is sweet, tender, subtle, soft, gentle, and you
    in the purest movement.
The wonders are within your beautiful soul.
The connection to God abides in the soul.

Prayer to God is not just a hope of change.
It's a solid communication with God.

An earnest prayer made in sincerity is neither given nor received
    lightly.
It is given the respect with which it was sent.
The opening of the heart can begin through the feeling in the soul.

God hears all pleas, all prayers, and all thankfulness, not only those
    given with word or thought
but also prayers given with feelings.

Forgiveness

Forgiving all who have done harm to you
exalts the soul. Let go of the fears, the hates, and
the despondency binding you to lower levels.

Bless those who have hurt you, for they
are the needy. You will feel the pains fall
from your soul. Your entire demeanor will lighten.
Why spend moments of self-proclaimed agony
when the same moments can bring joyousness?

Prayer for Life Extension

It may be that one may pray for the extension of
life for another. The soul's life has been predetermined
and agreed before birth on Earth. The prayers may
ease the suffering or may ease the lifting of the soul
by softening the fears of the soul.
The time may be correct to leave Earth
so that the prayers of love will surround the soul.
Death is a natural movement of the soul.

The will of God supersedes the will of mortals.
The soul may be needed in another place.
The work on Earth may have been fulfilled.
Many factors affect this outcome.

The basic life plan is not without pains.
Would you want the soul to remain in a diseased body?
Many times the prayer will help
not to keep the soul on Earth but to send love
to make the lifting easier. It is true: Prayer can heal
the body and raise the deceased again in a body,
but those on Earth are to let the soul lift to God,
    if it be decreed.
The ways of God are not always understood by men.

Helping the World through Prayer

The mass of intellect on Earth will override the ignorance of the
    lesser soul.
To achieve this, each soul must be worthy of self-love.
Each must be able to send love through thought communication.
Each must be able to lift the quality of thought to communicate
    with beings of a heavenly scope.
The world is in a tender state.
There must be intelligence on Earth.
The world must now be given the words of angels.
The souls of Earth are to evolve, each within themselves, to be the
    most wonderful and most intelligent souls possible.

Intellect begins the self-journey to lift to their highest beings.
Each soul is to begin a prayer to God, asking to help lift itself and
    the world from despondency, evil, and pain.
To lift to the angels and to the one great God,
    only a desire is needed.

Ask with a sincere heart. The angels know the sincerity of your soul.
The angels know the love, the fears — all that is you.
If each soul asked for help, all the intelligence in all the worlds and
    in all the heavens would rush to help.
Miracles of great multitudes would occur.
The thoughts of men are at varied levels, lingering in the
    atmosphere of the Earth.
If the lowest levels ceased to exist and higher levels of thought
permeated Earth, what wonders would occur! The wonders of the
heavens might be seen on Earth!

Lift the quality of your thought.
The creation of love can be cultivated in the mind.
Send love to any other being. To do this, feel the love with all the
emotion.
Focus this love to send to another.

The mind thinks of the happiness of the self.
To put the welfare of another before oneself, even in a small way,
is a way of giving love to another.
The most important reason for doing this is, of course,
the soul's growth but also the preservation of humankind.

The world is now to meet in group prayer where each person in the
world speaks to God from the heart.
This will enact miraculous results.

The world needs this prayer summit to help the world ignorance
and escalating hatred.
Not only are the leaders to meet, but all should arrange the moment
when all souls pray in unison to God.
The prayer of the souls should include:
freedom from ignorance,
freedom from fear,
wisdom for leaders of countries throughout the world,
prosperity and abundance,
the elimination of poverty, and
love and peacefulness throughout the world.

These are not only words.
This is to be felt deeply, fully in the soul.
This will help in many ways all over the world.

Miracles

Events may be altered. In an instant, creative change may occur to
    permeate wonder on Earth.
Miracles are what these manifestations are called.
These interventions are not a normal occurrence.
The movement of all things surrounding must be altered.
This is to occur if it is decided this is the best way to enact change.

All prayers are taken into account and discussed among the angels.
There are times when angels see a traumatic occurrence as the best
    way to help.
This is rare, but it does happen that a league of angels may
    intervene in a situation.

Angels love to work in subtle ways and movements.
Much thought is given to each action.
Angels enter the sphere of Earth so gently that
    they are almost undetected
until one is capable of feeling the surrounding love
    and can understand it comes from of the angels.

Though we are always with you, we are not always on Earth.
We are now in a place of great thought. This, in terms of Earth,
is a sacred place of the magnificent wisdom of God.
Here, we meet to take the prayers of people into account.
We listen and respond to prayers of the heart.
Should a prayer be in accordance with God's will, it is given
    as requested.
We would like to explain the most interesting way miracles
    conduce.

If the people of Earth pray, each in their own way,
    for a particular occurrence to come about,
we meet to discuss how this can be accomplished.
Not only do the people sending this thought into the atmosphere
    help the accomplishment of this goal,
but angels direct the outcome.
Working together, we and the people of Earth can bring
about the most wondrous conditions.

If one asks God with a humble, sincere heart, the prayer is taken
    most seriously in our chambers.
Wonders on Earth can occur in this way.
As it is, the minds of people are not focused into positive goals for
    humankind.
Everyone is selfishly thinking how to better themselves or to receive
    gifts.
Once the minds of humanity think beyond their own desires and
    concentrate on what is needed to help the world,
we angels rush in to help achieve this goal.

Miracles are a way of exacting specific results when other natural
    movements do not effect change.
The movements are to be explained by natural laws of Earth.
Not all circumstances of Earth are flexible enough to incorporate
the enactment of things beyond natural phenomena.

If the only possible way to bring change is through miraculous
    events, we angels convene to discuss
whether a miracle should be given.
Live any and every moment. Love all entities.
Become one with nature. All is energy.
The life force or soul within is energy on a level with God.
The miracles of God are wonders on Earth.

Blessings

Blessings are a desire to bring wonderment to someone
    other than yourself.
This is a selfless act that not only brings benefit to others
    but glorifies you beyond measure.

When you bring blessings to another,
you open your heart to feelings:
to love, to compassion, to empathy, to strength.

Blessings are not to be done only by those who feel
    authorized to perform this action.
You are to give blessings to God, to the angels,
    to all who surround you, to all beings, and to specific beings.

This is to be performed as you have the authority of God
within your soul. Healing blessings are often prepared by invoking
    the powers of God and healing entities
and by purifying the body by cleanliness and by fasting.

One need only to look at a person, feel what they are feeling,
and ask God to instill in you the power of the heavens
    to give blessings to the person.
You are focusing intense love and sending it to this person.

Bless God.
Bless all heavenly creatures.
Bless all entities of all worlds.
Bless your loved ones, your friends, your enemies, or anyone who
    has ever done harm to you.

Forgive them and bless them for, of all entities,
    they need the blessing the most.
They need your thoughts of tenderness and love.

Give them the blessings from your own powerful heart.
Send them thoughts of love and forgiveness from your mind.

Now you will understand how the blessing you send will free you
    and help you lift toward God.
You will know the power within your own soul.
You will see the love manifest before you.
A strength you may never have been aware will come forth.
You may see the transformations before you.

Don't think for a moment that you don't have the power to send
    love and blessings to another.
You have this power naturally bestowed by God in your being.

By blessing those around you, you are using a similar method
    to the works of angels.
By sending this love to even enemies, you are bringing
forgiveness and thanksgiving into the mind and heart,
    invoking wonders in life.

Receiving Desires: Prayer Type 1

Should the prayer be for material satisfaction,
One may wait a long time to receive it, or
it may not be given.

This is the lowest of prayers.
The worth of it is lowly.

All desires are given in the heavens.
The desire is not a necessity on Earth as it's only a fleeting
    fulfillment.
Temporary fulfillment gives no growth to the soul.
One is to give this life to the growth of the soul,
not to obtaining as much wealth as possible.

There is a particular type of soul growth one can obtain
on Earth through the senses of the physical body
that cannot be obtained outside the physical.
Life on Earth is so important for this development.
The length of time spent in a human body differs with each soul,
depending on what is needed in this life.

Much growth can be obtained in a moment or it may take a lifetime.
This type of prayer is without merit.

If you could ask God of one thing,
would you actually wish for temporary satisfaction?
This would reflect the lowest type of intelligence.
Give worth instead to attributes of the soul
    that live beyond the physical body.

The word prayer is not to be confused with methods of
    self-gratification.
Things are of no importance.
If things are used as a reason for prayer,
    they are often dismissed as not valid.

Does this mean prayers for material possessions are not answered?
We want all wonder for our charges on Earth, for all happiness to
    envelop the soul.
This is as much as a mother dreams for her child.

It's not necessary to possess material things in this life,
    for all will be given in the next life.
We will weigh the prayers for possession.
If it's necessary for the growth of the soul,
    it will be given.
The purpose of this life is not to gain all money
    and material possessions.
It's to help others and to evolve the soul.

The most beneficial results come from the sincerity
    found in an honest prayer.

Letting go of problems and giving them to God
    or to Jesus will lift the soul.
Knowing all will be taken care of will now open the way to the
    heart of the soul.

Attributes: Prayer Type 2

A prayer to gain a higher intelligence,
a more caring heart, compassion, and the love of kindness
     attracts angels to your side.
These prayers are of a higher level and are given if asked.
The plea is given from the soul as a sincere request.
The lifting of the soul to God begins with this quest.

At this point in the development of the soul,
one is wanting to open the heart to bring himself closer to God.
This is a sincere desire to become a better person.
Angels are always with you, but on hearing these pleas,
     they rush to your side.

In a contemplative state,
one may feel intense love surrounding the soul.
The level of growth will bear the light of the soul
     to all entities, in all worlds, and in all heavens.
The unveiling of the soul's light begins with the realization
of the soul that growth toward God is of much importance.

The quality of thought, of speech, and of action is purposely performed.
The prayers reflect this state of growth.
The material considerations are no longer desired.
The qualities of the soul are pleaded with God to achieve.
This is a good prayer.

Life is aware of the attributes it must obtain.
Let no person or any organization keep you from these attainments.

Homage to God: Prayer Type 3

The third type of prayer is the homage to God.
God is all-powerful and all-merciful.
To truly open the heart of the soul,
to bear the nakedness of the torrents of love,
to direct this to God in a tribute of blessing, of cherishing, and
of complete giving of oneself to God in absolute devotion
    is to bare the self to God.

The thankfulness one feels is now directed to God.
To bless him as he blesses you is a loving tribute.
This must be given in the most humble manner.
This is gratitude felt in the deepest parts of the soul.

This is to be performed in the aloneness of the soul,
as it is a sincere communication between the soul and
    the one, the holy God.
No viewing is to be given in the performance of this act.
Not one soul is to be in audience,
as this is a sole prayer between you and your God.

The soul is always protected.
The angels surround this most sacred communication
    of the most tender, vulnerable soul, speaking to the most
    sacred, holy God.
This prayer is not a request but a giving of love in
    completed thankfulness.
This is a prayer of the most high.

Helping Others: Prayer Type 4

The most important of all prayers is directed at helping others
beside yourself. If a prayer is for world peace or to
help others, it's a most honorable prayer.
This is most difficult for the souls of Earth
as the attention is on the quest for the happiness of the self.

To sincerely feel the pain of others and give your hopes
for them instead of yourself is a prayer given the highest worth.
Most mortals are not capable of this depth of feeling.
The surfacing wish is for the goodness to benefit oneself.

The Highest Way to Pray

This way to pray is called "integral."
You now use prayer in verbal communication and
    through silent thought.
The way of integral prayer is to weld with angels.
This is done by complete relaxation and asking the angels
to merge with you so you can comprehend all their thoughts and
    feelings.

This takes much time to integrate.
One is to let oneself relax into a meditation or almost a slumber.
Make the request and experience the angels merging.
This is done when one has time to experience this,
    as it is not done swiftly.
Integral prayer is another way to reach God through prayer.
This is not done when waking into action.
This is done in quietness, aloneness, and humbleness.

This prayer is more difficult, as it takes preparation of pulling oneself
    into a state of respect and reverence.
This is a method of closeness with the heavenly angels.
It is a total relaxation of the body and mind into a
meditative state, then a realization of the state and
a communication with the heavenly entities.

What wonders can occur from this prayer!
One may have visions of the future or know
    the thoughts of humanity.
Many truths are revealed if this is done repetitiously and
    in great reverence.

The integral prayer is a way of communing with the gods and the
    angels.
Even souls of the lowliest Earth can do this.

Sit. Let the mind relax as if sleep were coming.
Ask the angels to weld with you, as your mind delves deeper into
    the pure essence of the soul.
Ask the desire with a most humble heart.

The body will be a vessel to enact the powers of the gods and
    angels.
Let this be replicated once or twice daily, if possible.
This prayer will evoke many truths and wonders.

This is most sacred of all the types of prayer to God.
This takes a discipline and a giving of oneself.
The measure of the soul is brought forth for the viewing of the
    gods.
The sacredness of this communication will be noted by all heavenly
    beings.
The moments of welding with the higher entities are to be
    cherished.
This is a most sacred growth of the soul.
When the prayer is finished, arise and give thanks.

People of Earth are to know prayer can bring the world to
    peacefulness, even in this war-torn world.
If each soul desired a world of no war, no anger, and no hate, this
    would come about.
One prayer can change the entire world,
can speed or slow time,
can change the predetermined destiny of humankind.
This can be done by a single prayer.

Much care is to be given to bring wonders to all humanity.
The power of thought is more than those on Earth can imagine.

The people of Earth will one day realize this and develop
the thought function.

The utilization of the power of thought will occur when people
have evolved enough to use this for the benefit of humankind.
Humans are in an embryonic stage of development.
Wonders will occur on Earth when this power of thought
    is used constructively.

Life on Earth becomes more wonderful as the soul, the heart,
    and the mind integrate in people.

Such power is in you to accomplish greatness.
Begin by opening your soul to God.
Ask him to help you receive his love.
This will be given to you.

Ask God to lift you from ignorance.
This will be given. Ask him to let you feel kindness,
    compassion, love, and tenderness.
This will be given.

Humanity is awaiting the wonders of growing to God.
This will open an aliveness to blossom again on Earth.
This all begins with your thoughts, your prayers,
and the opening of your soul's heart.
Now is the time to lift to God.

About the Author

Cheryl Gaer Barlow has been communicating with angels most of her life. She attests that the first holy angel of God she ever saw floated through her window to appear before her in an intense blue-white light. The angel spoke to her, reached out to touch her forehead, and spoke to her. This was neither a dream nor a vision but a genuine visit from an angel of God.

"We give you the most powerful words given to any mortal," the angels told Cheryl on a subsequent visit. Cheryl was told she had been chosen to bring the words of the holy angels of God to Earth and that this was the reason she had been born on the planet at this time. "There's no trace of anything occult about this," she says. "I feel the angels beside me, dictating the words. They made clear that they are not disembodied spirits but truly hold the light of God."

Knowing she was part of something spiritual and significant, Cheryl wrote down the words of the angels exactly as she received them, regardless of her own beliefs. The messages Cheryl received were wise, informed, and uplifting, and they solidified the truth of her experience. The angels gave Cheryl not only words but also immense feelings and perceptions. "I then understood how the soul integrates with the intellect to determine the quality of thought and thus the quality of the soul," she explains. "I felt a refining and a softening into a tenderness I'd never before experienced. I have one foot in the heavens and one on Earth."

Cheryl enjoys living in a small New Mexico town with her husband — an ex-cowboy and an ex-U.S. Marshal — along with their dog, their cat, and their horse. In addition to communing with the angels, her other passions include painting and bronze sculpting.

ꙮ *Light Technology* PUBLISHING

BY DRUNVALO MELCHIZEDEK

LIVING IN THE HEART

Includes a CD with Heart Meditation

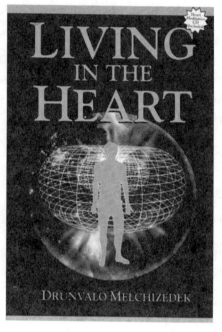

"Long ago we humans used a form of communication and sensing that did not involve the brain in any way; rather, it came from a sacred place within our hearts. What good would it do to find this place again in a world where the greatest religion is science and the logic of the mind? Don't I know this world where emotions and feelings are second-class citizens? Yes, I do. But my teachers have asked me to remind you who you really are. You are more than human being, much more. For within your heart is a place, a sacred place, where the world can literally be remade through conscious cocreation. If you give me permission, I will show you what has been shown to me."

Chapters Include:

- Beginning with the Mind
- Seeing in the Darkness
- Learning from indigenous Tribes
- The Sacred Space of the Heart
- The Unity of Heaven and Earth
- Leaving the Mind and Entering the Heart
- The Sacred Space of the Heart Meditation
- The Mer-Ka-Ba and the Sacred Space of the Heart
- Conscious Cocreation from the Heart Connected to the Mind

$25.00 Softcover, 120 PP.
ISBN 978-1-891824-43-2

Drunvalo Melchizedek's life experience reads like an encyclopedia of breakthroughs in human endeavor. He studied physics and art at the University of California at Berkeley, but he feels that his most important education came after college. In the past twenty-five years, he has studied wizh over seventy teachers from all belief systems and religious understandings. For some time now, he has been bringing his vision to the world through the Flower of Life program and the Mer-Ka-Ba meditation. This teaching encompasses every area of human understanding, explores the development of humankind from ancient civilizations to the present time, and offers clarity regarding the world's state of consciousness and what is needed for a smooth and easy transition into the twenty-first century.

Shifting Frequencies

with CD

Sounds for Vibratory Activation

by Jonathan Goldman

Now, for the first time, Healing Sounds pioneer Jonathan Goldman tells us about shifting frequencies — how to use sound and other modalities to change vibrational patterns for both personal and planetary healing and transformation. Through his consciousness connection to Shamael, Angel of Sound, Jonathan shares his extraordinary scientific and spiritual knowledge and insights, providing information, instructions, and techniques on using sound, light, color, visualization and sacred geometry to experience shifting frequencies. The material in this book is both timely and vital for health and spiritual evolution.

In this book, you will:
- Explore the use of sound in ways you never imagined for healing and transformation.
- Discover harmonics as a key to opening to higher levels of consciousness.
- Learn about the angel chakra and what sounds may be used to activate this new energy center.
- Find out how to transmute imbalanced vibrations using your own sounds.
- Experience the secrets of crystal singing.

Chapters Include:
- Sound Currents: Frequency and Intent
- Vibratory Resonance
- Vocalization, Visualization, and a Tonal Language
- The Harmonics of Sound
- Vocal Harmonics and Listening
- Energy Fields
- Creating Sacred Space
- Compassion through Sound
- Sound, Color, and Light
- Sound and Crystals
- Crystal Singing
- Breath
- The Waveform Experience
- Harmony
- Healing
- The Language of Light

$17.95 | ISBN 978-1-891824-70-8
Softcover, 226 pp.

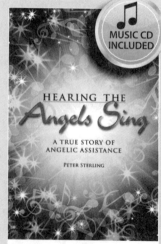

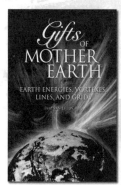

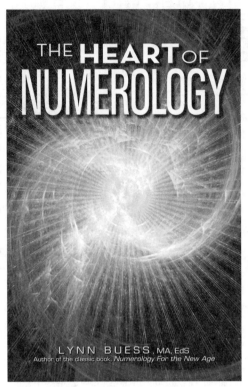

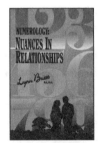

⚜ *Light Technology* PUBLISHING

TOM T. MOORE

THE GENTLE WAY
A SELF-HELP GUIDE FOR THOSE WHO BELIEVE IN ANGELS

This book is for all faiths and beliefs with the only requirement being a basic belief in angels. It will put you back in touch with your guardian angel or strengthen and expand the connection that you may already have. How can I promise these benefits? Because I have been using these concepts for over ten years and I can report these successes from direct knowledge and experience. But this is a self-help guide, so that means it requires your active participation.

$14.⁹⁵ • 160 PP. SOFTCOVER • ISBN 978-1-891824-60-9

THE GENTLE WAY II
BENEVOLENT OUTCOMES: THE STORY CONTINUES

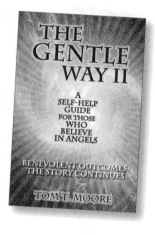

You'll be amazed at how easy it is to be in touch with guardian angels and how much assistance you can receive simply by asking. This inspirational self-help book, written for all faiths and beliefs, will explain how there is a more benevolent world that we can access, and how we can achieve this.

These very unique and incredibly simple techniques assist you in manifesting your goals easily and effortlessly for the first time. It works quickly, sometimes with immediate results — no affirmations written intentions, or changes in behavior are needed. You don't even have to believe in it for it to work!

$16.⁹⁵ • 320 PP. SOFTCOVER • ISBN 978-1-891824-80-7

THE GENTLE WAY III
MASTER YOUR LIFE

Almost three years have passed since *The Gentle Way II* was published. Yet as many success stories as that book contained, I have continued to receive truly unique stories from people all over the world requesting most benevolent outcomes and asking for benevolent prayers for their families, friends, other people, and other beings. It just proves that there are no limits to this modality, which is becoming a gentle movement as people discover how much better their lives are with these simple yet powerful requests.

$16.⁹⁵ • 352 PP. SOFTCOVER • ISBN 978-1-62233-005-8

Print books: visit our online bookstore www.LightTechnology.com
eBooks available on Amazon, Apple iTunes, Google Play, and Barnes & Noble

♦ Light Technology PUBLISHING

Dr. Joshua David Stone's
Easy-to-Read Encyclopedia of the Spiritual Path

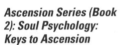
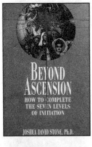

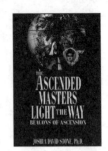

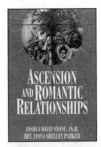
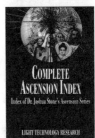